CW00739932

JAMES RAVILIOUS

A LIFE

JAMES RAVILIOUS
A LIFE

ROBIN RAVILIOUS

WILMINGTON SQUARE BOOKS
An imprint of
BITTER LEMON PRESS

WILMINGTON SQUARE BOOKS
An imprint of Bitter Lemon Press

First published in 2017 by
Wilmington Square Books
47 Wilmington Square
London WC1X 0ET

www.bitterlemonpress.com

A CIP record for this book is available from the
British Library

ISBN 978-1-908524-942
ISBN (pb) 978-1-912242-160

4 6 8 9 7 5 3

Designed and typeset by Jane Havell Associates
Printed in China

FRONTISPIECE
Portrait of James Ravilious, 1970s
Unknown photographer

For Ben and Ella

CONTENTS

PROLOGUE

RAVILIOUS: as a child, I found that intriguing word written on the back of some of our specimen Wedgwood dinner plates at home. I used to think it was an adjective. Then, one evening in May 1969, I came across it again. I was hovering shyly at a party in London given by some cousins of mine when I was introduced to a group of young men; one of them was a James Ravilious. The plates gave me something to talk about.

In front of me stood a slim, six-foot man with large gentle eyes like a Guernsey cow. I noted a long angular face with a high forehead and a Pre-Raphaelite chin, on an unusually long neck for a man. He talked in an eager gabble which was hard to follow, but he was clearly friendly. When I made a move to go he offered to share a taxi. By the end of the short ride to my borrowed flat in Bayswater his arm had slid around my waist. I thought him a fast worker, but amiable – if slightly mad.

A few days later he gave me lunch at Bertorelli's restaurant in Queensway, and I began to learn the difficult art of conversing with a grasshopper. For James's speaking style was quite eccentric in those days. He would jump from subject to subject without any signals, leaving a sentence not merely unfinished, but trailing off in a trickle of unintelligible sounds as his mind leapt on. At times the main subject word was missing altogether and one had to run, mentally, to keep up. But he was warm, and funny, and although almost thirty, engagingly boyish. I liked the way he treated the waiter as an equal; and I liked the interest he took in me – my life, my past. In all my twenty-four years I had never had any one I felt safe to talk to about personal things. With James it was suddenly easy. He saw straight through to the unconfident, unfocused, self-conscious girl inside, and saw with sympathy. I found it curiously restful. I soon discovered that he and I had travelled similar roads, both of us growing up in the shadow of distinguished artistic forebears (four of whom had died in their prime), whose standards of excellence in their various arts seemed dauntingly beyond our reach. Both of us knew well the complicated feeling, half-proud, half-depressing, when strangers recognised our names and connections. Both of us had often had to field that difficult question, explicit or implied: 'So what are *you* going to do?'

1 . JAMES'S CHILDHOOD

JAMES'S CHEERFUL EAGERNESS belied a far from easy childhood of disruption and loss; by the age of twelve he had lost both his parents, lived in five different homes, and attended four different boarding schools.

He was born in an Eastbourne nursing home on 22 August 1939, two weeks before war was declared. His parents, Eric and Tirzah, had come from rather different drawers of Eastbourne society. Tirzah's father, Lieutenant Colonel Frederick Garwood, had been a professional soldier in the Royal Engineers in India. A great letter writer and an amateur photographer, he had a dry sense of humour, especially about his four daughters. Tirzah, the third one, was his favourite. Her mother, Ella, from the well-to-do Belfast shipping family of Corry, was a highly organised doer of good works (though she painted and embroidered flowers very competently in what spare time she had). She was a firm disciplinarian. Both of them cared a lot about social status.

Eric's family, however, was 'in trade'. His father, Frank Ravilious, who came from Tonbridge in Kent, had been in the furniture making and upholstery business, having trained initially in his brother's coach-building works, and then run small antique shops, first in Acton, later in Eastbourne. Frank was an impulsive, irascible man, an eccentric evangelist given to religious visions, and to accosting visitors with tracts and blunt enquiries about the health of their souls – not an easy father. The family was held together by Eric's much-loved mother Emma, a West Country girl, daughter of William Ford, agricultural labourer and gardener, of Kingsbridge in South Devon. Eric was embarrassed by his father, and never took friends home. He moved up in the world on his artistic talent, winning scholarships first to Eastbourne School of Art, and then to the Design School of the Royal College of Art, where he was taught by Paul Nash among others, and where he made lifelong friendships with fellow students such as Edward Bawden, Douglas Percy Bliss, Barnett Freedman, Enid Marx and Peggy Angus. He returned to Eastbourne to teach design and wood-engraving at the art school, and it was there, in 1926, that Tirzah Garwood became his most promising pupil. Highly susceptible to pretty girls, Eric soon fell for her pale-skinned dark-eyed beauty and her vivacious way of talking. After some indecision, Tirzah rejected a safe middle-class admirer, and in 1930 she married Eric. It took her parents a while to come round to her choice of husband. An attractive but rather raffish-looking arty fellow from the wrong side of the tracks, and with no reliable prospects, was not what they had had in mind for her – especially as his family had been involved in a well-publicised bankruptcy case in the town a few years earlier.

The couple went to live for a while in London, where Eric got a new teaching job. In 1932, yearning for landscape, they joined Edward and Charlotte Bawden in renting part of Brick House in the Essex village of Great Bardfield for country breaks. Both Eric and Edward had been excited by the Victoria & Albert Museum's first big exhibition of the artist Samuel Palmer in 1926, and had searched for special countryside to inspire them as Shoreham in Kent had inspired him. At Brick House, while Eric engraved, Tirzah exper-

Eric Ravilious and Tirzah Garwood's
engagement photo, Eastbourne, 1930

imented with marbling paper, creating in subtle Thirties colours delicately controlled designs that have never been equalled. The Bawdens and Raviliouses became fond of that part of Essex, which was sprinkled with attractive villages of timber-framed or eighteenth-century brick houses, and still quite countrified in the pre-war era. So fond that both couples decided to settle there. Eric and Tirzah moved into Bank House, a small Georgian brick building in nearby Castle Hedingham in 1934. They were sociable and hospitable, and made many creative friends, for the area was becoming an artistic colony. They were based there when all three of their children were born: John in 1935, James in 1939, and Anne in 1941.

Also in 1934, Eric caught up with fellow Royal College of Art student Peggy Angus, who was now teaching at Eastbourne College of Art. She invited him and Tirzah to Furlongs, the Victorian flint-and-brick farm cottage she had recently discovered near Glynde in Sussex. Unmodernised, and up a long muddy farm track, it was surrounded by sweeping cornfields and the sensual forms of the South Downs. Furlongs was cheap, and enticingly remote – an inspiring place for creative people. Peggy would rent half of it as a holiday home for the rest of her life, filling it with friends willing to forgo comfort for an exhilarating sense of freedom, artistic and personal. It rapidly became a fruitful place for art and for love affairs.

Eric was to make good use of it. Up till then, apart from a couple of murals, he had mainly been working in black and white, and on a small scale, doing wood engravings in which his talent as a designer was paramount. But now he was beginning to enjoy painting in watercolour as well. Furlongs and its surroundings offered inviting new subjects: a cement works, old machinery and greenhouses, the cottage itself, inside and out – everyday things which he painted with an attention that gave them an almost surreal clarity – while the grand curves and textures of downland inspired a strong new approach to landscape.

Furlongs was also a place where he could meet his new lover Helen Binyon, Peggy's London flatmate, who was a daughter of Laurence Binyon, the poet, art historian and Keeper of Oriental Prints and Drawings at the British Museum. Helen was artistic too, and would later become an innovative puppeteer and a teacher at the Bath Academy of Art at Corsham. She admired Eric's work enormously and, unencumbered by domestic cares, was an appreciative and enthusiastic companion at a time when Tirzah was worn out by domesticity. Eric told Tirzah about the affair, and very nearly left her at one point; but with honesty and tolerance the marriage survived, and they went on to have James, the child of their reconciliation, followed by Anne. Later, Tirzah would describe Eric as 'the kindest' of the men in her life, so she had clearly forgiven him. When the affair was over, Helen Binyon remained a close friend of Eric; they corresponded regularly for the rest of his life, his many vivid letters to her shedding light on him and his work.

At this time, one of Eric's preoccupations was the lithographed illustrations for a book for the Curwen Press called *High Street*. He collaborated on it with Peggy Angus's new husband, architectural writer J. M. Richards, who later became editor of *The Architectural Review*. It was a collection of portraits of shops which they had found in Essex and London: old-world establishments with fine lettering and idiosyncratic goods elegantly displayed.

Meanwhile, his painting career was taking off. His watercolours, many of them of Sussex, had been very successful in an exhibition at Zwemmer's in 1936, and he began to travel about to other paintable locations: the Black Mountains, the Kent coast, and the ports of Bristol and Normandy. He also began a series of pictures of the great chalk figures of southern Britain. Like so many fellow artists, he was recording the everyday England he loved as the growing threat from an aggressive Germany made it ever more precious. When war broke out, this work earned him an invitation from Kenneth Clark to be an official War Artist.

Eric seems always to have been quite free from the angst which besets a lot of artists. He enjoyed his work. As a War Artist, he enjoyed it even more. He was a born recorder, and on assignments to docks at Chatham, Sheerness and Grimsby, and on manoeuvres off Norway in a destroyer with the Atlantic convoys, his posts (Honorary Captain, Royal Marines, and later in the RAF) gave him access to fascinating worlds where he could make pictures of the technology of the time: coastal defences, warships, submarines, Lysanders and Spitfires. He developed his remarkable skill for reducing a complex machine to its simplest form, while also continuing to paint the landscapes he loved, now wearing their wartime dress, and to explore new effects in sea- and cloudscapes. Now, even more, his subjects gained a surreal quality – intensely observed and enjoyed, and portrayed in a clear, almost dreamlike, light which, in the originals, shines out from the paper, a quality seldom achieved in watercolour. All are distinguished by his sense of design and composition, and by a boyish zest that gives little hint of the fear or gloom of war, or of the dangerous situations (he called them 'excitements') that he was sometimes in while painting them.

Back home in Essex, life was rather less enjoyable for Tirzah. The savage winter of 1940 froze the pipes at Bank House; they later burst and flooded the ground floor, which never fully recovered. Shortly after Anne's birth, the Raviliouses moved a few miles away to a small farmhouse in the parish of Shalford. It belonged to the MP John Strachey, who asked for half of the rent to be paid in paintings by Eric. But it was not a hugely practical move, for here too there were many domestic problems. Ironbridge Farm was an old half-timbered Essex farmstead full of appealing character but near – too near – the River Pant. The boys would remember it with affection, but it was only really habitable in summer, and quite remote – a taxing place in which to bring up young children. Damp was again a problem, and cold, the regular freezing and bursting of the pipes knocked out the cooking range and the hot water boiler together. The simple life, though inspiring, was not all that simple; and a colonel's daughter would not perhaps have had much experience of the basics of housework.

The drudgery was hard on her. She had to shelve her own talents almost completely. Her health had never been robust at the best of times. Now everyone was run down by the cold, the stress, and the restricted diet of wartime, and the children were often ill. Kind friends rallied round, and she employed local girls as nursemaids when she could, while her mother, by now almost seventy, went so often to cope with the various crises, in great discomfort, that her husband dryly christened her 'the Eastbourne Lifeboat'.

But if things had not been easy before, in 1942 they got far worse for poor Tirzah. In the previous winter, the children had been seriously ill with whooping cough. In the early spring she was diagnosed with breast cancer, and had to have one breast removed, leaving her unable to lift the children for some time. Soon after, James got measles and had to be segregated from one-year-old Anne. All this was of course in the context of war. Tirzah wrote a depressed letter to John Strachey, her landlord, cataloguing the domestic problems, but ending, 'Of course, the invasion may come and it won't matter very much either way.'

A month or so later she discovered she was pregnant again and, though she would have liked another child, she was advised to have a termination. Eric was seldom at home to support her, as he was being posted all over Britain on War Artist assignments. Then, in late August, soon after she returned from a second hospital stay, he set off eagerly for a four-month trip to paint the work of the RAF's Norwegian squadron stationed in the extraordinary graphic landscape of Iceland. On his fifth day there, he took off from Kaldadarnes airfield on an Air-Sea Rescue mission to hunt for an aircraft which had disappeared, and his plane was also lost without trace.

James was just three when Eric left home for Iceland; his only memory of his father was of running down the lane that summer morning to say goodbye to him, and of Eric giving him a hug and a threepenny bit.

After the telegram announcing Eric's disappearance, Tirzah existed for a while in limbo. She mourned for him, but he could not be declared dead officially until he had been missing for six months, though his pay had been stopped. Because he had been non-combatant, it took the best part of a year for the powers that be to decide that she was eligible for a war widow's pension. The children were adding to her troubles. John, aged seven, had asthma and was being bullied in the village school, while the younger two were, according to their grandfather, running wild. 'Anne and James very unruly and noisy,' he noted in his diary. 'Tirzah never tells them off.'

Exhausted, grieving, and short of money, she struggled on at Ironbridge Farm with what help friends and her mother could give. That winter James spent several months alone with his grandparents in Eastbourne (where his confident chattiness was approved), Tirzah and the baby joining him after Christmas when John went back to school. But there were frequent hit-and-run raids on the town: mortar and air attacks on the nearby railway station, which came so suddenly there was barely time for the sirens to sound. Grandpa Garwood wrote of the problems, familiar to many, of rushing small children out of their cots and down to the precarious shelter of the cellar.

James kept no frightening wartime memories, but he was quite shocked by sudden loud noises all his life. What he did remember, from a visit to Furlongs in the summer of 1944, was the thrilling sight of the whole sky above the Downs filled edge to edge with gliders on their way to France. It must have been 5 June, when they would have been going to drop paratroops ahead of the D-Day landings next morning. Coincidentally, only ten miles away in Brighton, my uncle Rex Whistler, a successful painter, muralist and illustrator who had moved in some of the same circles as Eric, was waiting with his tank troop to embark for Normandy, and painting a saucy cartoon of the Prince

Regent on their billet wall to lift his fellow officers' spirits. Six weeks later Rex was killed by a German mortar shell on his first day in action. He was thirty-nine, the same age as Eric when he died.

After a while Tirzah moved from Ironbridge to a more convenient home, Boydells Farm, near Wetherfield, but things were still not easy, and she had little time for her work. But in 1945 she met Henry Swanzy, who became her second husband. He was lodging in Peggy Angus's London house, 122 Adelaide Road, Chalk Farm, while working for the Overseas Service of the BBC. He would soon become producer of its weekly radio programme, *Caribbean Voices*, doing much to bring West Indian writing into the canon of literature in English. Among others, he helped to launch V. S. Naipaul, who had just graduated from Oxford and was, in his own words, 'practically in the gutter'.[1] Henry encouraged his writing, and gave him a job presenting the programme. Henry was a warm, clever and enthusiastic man, well-read and voluble. He fell for Tirzah and she responded, though not before she had written him one of her characteristically frank letters warning him that she was seven years his senior, and had lost one breast. But her life was still complicated. To begin with, there were the logistics of travelling to and fro between Essex to London to help Henry set up a flat for his working week. Then there were the normal distractions of illnesses, dental appointments and school uniforms. On top of this they were still, like everyone else, on severe postwar rations, though Tirzah did her best to supplement these by raising poultry and growing vegetables. She wrote to Henry in the spring of 1946 on the hazards of keeping the children occupied in the holidays: John with cooking, James and Anne (aged six and four) with painting the greenhouse – at the end of which there was flour all over John, and white paint all over the younger two. 'What a life!' she wrote with humorous stoicism. 'My gawd, it's cold.'

Tirzah and Henry married in February 1946, and eventually the family united in London, in another house in Adelaide Road, no. 169 (now demol-

ished), a few doors from Peggy, where the artist Ivon Hitchens had been living. The hens came too, and supplied family and neighbours with eggs. So the next stage of the children's lives was based in a tall London villa with an overgrown garden above the railway cutting of the London, Midlands & Scottish Railway line. The house vibrated night and day when the big steam locomotives shunted in the tunnels below; its fabric had been severely shaken by the bombs that destroyed the building next door. The bomb site was the children's playground. To begin with, the house was infested with fleas and had to be fumigated. Later, the problem was mice. Tirzah's novel method of dealing with these was to plug their holes with putty. Next morning the holes had been reopened, and there were pale-coloured droppings all over the floors.

Anne now started school in Primrose Hill; the two boys were already at boarding school. In reaction to her own upbringing, Tirzah had been

James, Anne and John Ravilious with Peggy Angus's daughter
Victoria in the garden of 169 Adelaide Road, London, c. 1948
Edwin Smith/RIBA Collections

impressed by the doctrine of the reforming educationalist A. S. Neill, who advocated that children should be separated from the restricting influence of their parents as soon as possible, and allowed to learn whatever interested them, and to develop self-discipline and motivation at their own pace. Perhaps she didn't go that far, but she clearly thought it good for the children to be sent away. A Garwood uncle's legacy made it possible, so all three got a more expensive education than she could possibly have afforded otherwise. Both boys were around six when they were first sent to Cotter's Bow, a small boarding school near Burford in the Cotswolds. Edward Bawden's children, Richard and Joanna, were already there. It rescued John from the miseries of the rough village school in Essex, and James joined him in due course. James looks rather alone and vulnerable in his 1946 school photograh, but acclimatised better than some as he quite enjoyed communal life. Joanna Bawden,

Tirzah with James on the wall,
169 Adelaide Road, London, c. 1949
Edwin Smith/RIBA Collections

who had started there in wartime, vividly recalled the sound of sobbing every night in the pitch dark of a blacked-out dormitory, for many of the children had been abruptly parted from their parents by the London Blitz – sometimes forever. John and James were at Cotter's Bow until it shut down in 1948.

Meanwhile, life was kinder to Tirzah for a while. She was happy with Henry, who clearly adored her, and relieved to have found a kind and fun-loving stepfather for her children. Now at last she had time and energy to be an artist again. In the summer of 1946 she took the two boys for a carefree holiday on the tiny Hebridean island of Canna in company with the Gilbert Spencers and Helen Binyon, Eric's former lover, who had become her friend. It was one of James's happiest childhood memories. While Tirzah painted, he and John explored the shore and risked their necks on the cliffs. Tirzah's work was going well at this time, and she was able to see many old friends in London, such as artists Michael and Duffy Rothenstein, and Kenneth and Diana Rowntree, and to make new ones including the photographer Edwin Smith and his wife Olive Cook. Olive, a lovely, enthusiastic person, had worked under Kenneth Clark during the war as press officer responsible for keeping alive public awareness of the National Gallery's collection while it was in exile in a slate mine in Wales. In the 1950s she would work in harness with Edwin, writing scholarly texts for his books of superb architectural photography. Edwin took delightful pictures of Tirzah and her children.

But disturbing symptoms reappeared for Tirzah in 1948, and she was almost too weak to cope with a holiday in a B&B at Cromer that summer. The cancer had returned, and she was subjected to radium and hormone treatments which took their toll. In the summer of 1950 her doctors discovered secondary growth in her spine. There was nothing more they could do for her apart from primitive palliatives. She could not tolerate morphine. Eventually, the struggle to cope at Adelaide Road, even with the help of friends and a live-in housekeeper, became too much and she moved into a nursing home at

Copford Place, a pleasant manor house near Mark's Tey in Essex. It was possible for Henry to live there with her and to commute to London for his work, and the children could sometimes join her there in the school holidays.

Although Tirzah was not always bedridden in those last years, and could present a valiantly cheerful front despite her pain, family life became, of necessity, more and more disturbed. The children had to get used to being dispersed for the holidays, in various groupings, to relations or friends. Sometimes Peggy Angus took them down to Furlongs with her own two, Victoria and Angus, the children of her brief marriage to J. M. Richards. Christine Nash (wife of the artist John Nash) and Olive Cook also helped. Olive was childless; Christine had lost her only child in a tragic car accident; both were very fond of the Ravilious three. In term time there was still the epic organisation of getting them to three different boarding schools, for Anne had moved on to a tiny school at Aldeburgh, and John was at a progressive school, Long Dene, in Kent, the closure of Cotter's Bow having separated the two boys.

James had been sent to Dane Court School near Blandford in Dorset. Tirzah chose this as she had hopes of him moving on eventually to nearby Bryanston, a liberal school specialising in the arts. Richard Bawden was already at Dane Court, and enjoying it. James did well there, too. In his first few weeks, the headmaster reported to Tirzah that he was 'sensibly independent' and 'evidently enjoying his new life'. His teachers considered him artistic and academic. He was often near the top of his class. But as Tirzah wrote to Henry: 'I found from the Tuelys that it costs £210 a year at Bryanston. Our James will have to get scholarships if he wants to be a gentleman.' Dane Court School was in Whatcombe House, a large, rather stern-looking Georgian mansion set in beautiful rolling parkland – by far the most elegant house James ever lived in. He was surrounded by wrought-iron balustrades and Adam-style mantelpieces, and the classrooms had open fires. The school offered considerable freedom, and plenty of outdoor life, with lots of sports such as football and cricket, which James was good at; also enjoyable hobbies such as carpentry, bird-watching, camp-building and tree-climbing in the wooded part of the grounds known to the boys as Bunny Bump. By this time James was what my primary school teacher would have called 'a thoroughly normal little boy', keen on the radio serial *Dick Barton – Special Agent,* Meccano, balsa wood kits, comics, weedy jokes, and stodgy puddings with custard. Most of those interests would remain with him all his life in one form or another.

As always at boarding schools, the boys had to write home once a week. Several of James's letters have survived, the early ones to his mother, the later ones to Henry, recording typical schoolboy doings in a laborious round hand: 'Could I have a new stamp book. There is a bam-boo tree and you can go and get one and make a fishing rod. We are making a chiken house in carpentry.' Or 'We had lecture on Ancient Dorset arkieology and he showed us picturs on a magic lantern.' But James's growing anxiety about home is clear. All the later letters include the sentence, 'I hope Mummy is getting better.' It must have been an unsettling time for all three children, locked away in their separate school worlds, then returning for holidays in one household after another to catch perhaps only a glimpse of their mother each time, though poor Anne saw more than she was supposed to see.

A poignant little incident from near the end of this period was recorded by Olive Cook. She had volunteered to meet James off his end-of-term train. As she greeted the eleven-year-old hurrying towards her down the platform he asked, 'Is Mummy still alive?'

Tirzah died on Easter Tuesday, 27 March 1951, aged forty-two. Apparently James had been left at school over the holiday because of the situation, as often happened in those days. When he was actually told is difficult to establish. Certainly it appears to have been a normal school day, for he vividly remembered being called out of morning lessons to the office of the headmaster, who said, 'I'm sorry to tell you that your mother has died'; then returning to his classroom, numb and tearless. In the afternoon he took an exam. No one talked to him about it again. School went on as if nothing had happened.

It seems incredible these days that a child could be left to cope with bereavement alone in this way, but the culture of stiff upper lip prevailed. On the surface, James took his news well, and that was what mattered. What it did to a sensitive loving boy is impossible to know. Awareness in childhood of the fragility of human life has a profound effect, however well buried. Perhaps in the sealed-in world of boarding school he was insulated from grief and loss for a while. Certainly he would not have wanted to expose his feelings at all. I imagine that it was at this time that he learnt to protect himself by joking his way out of emotion, a trait he kept all his life. But his relationship with his mother had been close. He was known to be her favourite: the funny, friendly, talkative little boy with appealing calf eyes who was, in her words, 'the life and soul' of any gathering. Fellow students who knew him ten years later say he would take from his wallet for any sympathetic listener a last photograph of Tirzah by Edwin Smith. It was still there when I got to know him. It shows her in bed, worn by illness but still beautiful.

James was understandably partisan about his parents' marriage when he found out about it as an adult. He had vivid memories of his mother – for whom he had never really been able to grieve – while his father was little more than a name. Though he came to admire his work, James felt his father had dealt Tirzah a raw deal, and he was prejudiced against unfaithful husbands from then on. I'm sure he inherited his interest in people from his mother. Eric was undoubtedly a good companion, very popular with his friends, but not, it seems, particularly interested in people as such. Tirzah was definitely a 'people person': a shrewd observer of character and relationships. Before motherhood overtook her, she had made robust wood engravings poking affectionate fun, as Betjeman did, at the middle class from which she came: stout

ladies in brogues and tweeds at a dog show, sleek young men with their flapper girls at the bar. Like Eric's work, they show a relish for domestic detail and pattern, but she was better than her teacher at capturing people. She clearly found them fascinating.

I wish I had known her. I'm sure she would have been a lovely mother-in-law. She was humorous, liberal-minded, affectionate though quite unsentimental, plain-speaking and courageous. She believed in personal freedom, for her children, and for Eric. 'I accepted the fact that his work was more important to him than me,' she wrote, 'and I appreciated this attitude.' And she came to terms with his unfaithfulness. (She herself had a brief affair with the artist John Alderton, which brought her happiness and misery – the love lives of their circle were quite complicated.) Domestic cares were often in the way of her own considerable talent; and she struggled valiantly with widowhood, money worries and her own ill health. After her mastectomy, she began an autobiography that records in frank detail her relationships, Eric's working practice, and the lives of their circle of friends and relations, portraying them with an amused, though sometimes devastating, candour. When the cancer returned and she had again to endure the brutal treatments then prescribed, she made plans for her children's future without her, and sat up in bed producing mysterious, slightly surreal, oil paintings of toys and animals in garden settings or jolly little three-dimensional collages of houses in painted paper and card – finding genuine happiness in the chance to work freely at last, even though she knew perfectly well that her time was short.

Tirzah in bed at 169 Adelaide Road, London, 1950
Edwin Smith/RIBA Collections

By coincidence, I did actually meet her once, in 1949, when I was four. As she wrote to James at school: 'Sorry I haven't written before but we were in a very wild part of Devonshire . . . at a christening.' This was the christening, in the tiny hamlet of Dowland two miles from Addisford, our future home, of John and Katya Furse – the cousins who would eventually introduce James and me. Tirzah was there because Henry Swanzy was one of the godfathers. I can just recall the occasion, but unfortunately I don't remember her at all.

The Dog Show, 1929 (wood engraving)
Tirzah Garwood

2 . JAMES'S TEENAGE YEARS

TIRZAH'S DEATH meant big changes for the three orphans. Henry Swanzy could not manage his job and three stepchildren aged fifteen, eleven and nine, though he remained a most generous and affectionate stepfather for the rest of his life. Ella Garwood, aged seventy-nine, was their only surviving grandparent, and she would die the following year. So, as Tirzah had arranged, they were already based in Warwickshire with their new legal guardians, Henry's younger brother John Swanzy and his wife Kay. The children knew Kay; she and her previous husband, the designer and architect Robert Goodden, had become good friends and neighbours of the Raviliouses in Essex when they first moved to Castle Hedingham. She was unable to have children of her own. She and John were the only friends prepared to offer a home to all three young people together – a remarkable undertaking. Accordingly, the three moved into the Swanzys' house, Hopkins, in Long Marston, and into a milieu that was cultivated but not artistic. It was perhaps not unlike the world of their Garwood grandparents: a conventionally well-to-do middle class life of drinks

parties, tennis matches, hunt balls, and knowing the right people. John commuted to Alcester for his work with Millwards Needles, while Kay, who had been in the WAAF and worked in the Cabinet Office before becoming Education Organiser for the Federation of Women's Institutes, got involved in village life and lectured on literature at local WI meetings.

All thought of James aiming for Bryanston was now abandoned owing to distance, cost and a different ideology. Kay diligently researched schools for all three, and it was decided that James should be put down for Bedford School, an establishment traditionally favoured by military families, because John Swanzy had been there, and his mother still lived nearby. To achieve this, James was removed from Dane Court and sent to a crammer in Somerset to prepare for the Common Entrance exam. This was Glencot, a nineteenth-century neo-Jacobean mansion with a river running through the garden, near Wookey Hole. Again, James seems to have survived well enough to remember it with some affection, and to hold on to his sugar-pink cap as an amusing

John and Kay Swanzy at Hopkins,
Long Marston, Warwickshire, c. 1950

memento until he was in his fifties. On a photographic project in the nearby Mendips, he called in and found the house had become a hotel. He presented the cap to the proprietors for their collection of memorabilia.

In September 1952, he entered the imposing red-brick world of Bedford School and was allocated to Redburn House, in the care of house-master Richard Roseveare and his wife. The latter recalled James as 'a little lost', and was motherly to him. There was quite a friendly atmosphere in Redburn: the boys lived *en famille* with the Roseveares to some extent. But in general the school was a conventional institution then, with fagging, caning of boys by boys, and rigid discipline (the very opposite of what Tirzah had had in mind for him). The intention was still that school should toughen boys for the rigours of adult life – probably in the services – so physical hardship, and pain, a bit of bullying perhaps and relentless rules were all part of their educa-tion. The youngest, the 'ticks' and 'remnants', endured their way up through the hierarchy till they, in their turn, could lord it over the next generation. The dormitories were so cold – they were unheated, and the windows were not allowed to be shut – that the boys had to spread their overcoats on their beds in winter. Military-style training in the Combined Cadet Force was a part of life, and early morning cross-country runs; slovenly dress was punished; Chapel was obligatory twice on Sundays; daily curfew imposed at 6.30 p.m. sharp. The regime was not very successful with James, however. He conformed at the time, but it left him with a lifelong aversion to Church of England reli-gion, the military, and being told what to do.

Some of the teachers were wounded veterans of the Great War, and fairly eccentric. In later life, James, who was an excellent mimic, would dine out on tales of them, including the one with a wooden leg who used to shout 'Hold up your work, boy!' so that he could view it through binoculars from the comfort of his desk. David Heald, James's near contemporary, described the marksmanship of some of the masters in throwing a piece of chalk, or even a wooden blackboard duster, at an inattentive head.

The food was the usual institutional fare, but the boys assuaged their craving for the comfort of sweet things, as far as their pocket money would allow, by raiding the local shops for sweets, chocolate and, in James's case, cans of condensed milk to be scooped from the tin with a grubby finger. But he could at least escape on his bike for Sunday lunch with 'Granny Swanzy', John and Henry's mother, who lived not far from the school. She would feed him up, and cosset him.

It is hard to imagine James in a more unlikely setting, though he never spoke of it critically. His true personality seems to have been suppressed by what he had been through. Contemporaries remember him as friendly, but quiet and self-contained. Others even describe him as studious. They say he 'kept his head down and worked'. He did well in mathematics, but didn't distinguish himself in anything else, apparently – least of all art. Bedford taught him golf, snooker and chess, and how to shoot quite well with a .22 rifle, and allowed him time in the 'Playroom' to pursue the model-making which he still enjoyed. Like most public schools at that time, it fostered friendships with other boys, and firmly deprived him of any contact at all with that dangerous alien race, girls.

In the holidays the three siblings were together more than they had been for some time, and their lives became far more settled. They loved Hopkins, which was an old Cotswold stone house with irregular floors, outhouses, a garden and an orchard, set in the lush Warwickshire countryside – an inviting antidote to boarding school. The three were close, united by their shared loss. When James and Anne (who adored him) were not pedalling round the lanes together, Anne learned domestic skills from Kay, who was a good cook and very capable, while James did boyish things with his gifted elder brother John.

For the rest of their lives they would remain in touch, by phone and at family gatherings for Christmas and private views; and Anne would support both her brothers devotedly through all their troubles.

Although eccentric, and withdrawn in company, John was already an inventor, an experimental scientist, mostly self-taught, able to make a crystal radio that really worked, to trap methane from the duck pond and set it alight, or to design and construct a canvas canoe which they could launch on the nearby River Avon. He also introduced James to photography. Their darkroom was a cubbyhole under the stairs not much more than a metre each way, with a blanket to black out the door. Here the two of them huddled over the trays

Double exposure of James, c. 1952
John Ravilious

of noxious chemicals for hours – on all fours as there was no room to stand up. And here, not content with ordinary photos, they processed a remarkable double exposure: two rather ghostly Jameses shaking hands with each other. John was also talented at woodwork. He later trained in furniture-making at the Royal College of Art. James improved on his prep school carpentry by watching John at work in the old dairy at Hopkins. All three siblings were good with their hands, a legacy from the Ravilious side of the family perhaps, which had produced many craftsmen, furniture makers, upholsterers, coach-builders and carpenters, since Victorian times, as well as wood engraver Eric. A special affinity with wood was clearly a family trait. The boys also had a feeling for engineering which they may have inherited from their Garwood grandfather, the Royal Engineer.

The Swanzys' marriage was not a very happy one, but they were conscientious guardians, and remained warmly concerned in their wards' welfare after they grew up. John Swanzy, with his clipped, rather military manner, exacting standards and right-wing views, was perhaps a disappointed man, but enthusiastic about history and the countryside. Kay was kind and motherly, reading aloud to them in the evenings, and writing regularly to all three at school. Both John and Kay had degrees in English, John from Cambridge and Kay from Oxford, and took the young people's education seriously. There was intellectual talk at table for their benefit, and educational trips to Stratford-on-Avon and the continent. But their artistic heritage seems to have been allowed to fade from their minds. Their parents were never mentioned, and they were hardly aware of their father's work, or his growing reputation, having lost touch with Eric and Tirzah's artistic friends.

Teenaged James acclimatised to this lifestyle, attending any gathering of the Swanzys' set where there might be girls (to be wistfully looked at, never touched). He was more or less at ease socially at such gatherings, but I don't think he ever felt he belonged in that milieu. His sympathies were leftwing even then. He had grown the carapace of a public schoolboy, but deep down I think he always felt that it was to some extent a disguise.

The Bedford era came to an end in July 1957. James was nearly eighteen and, according to the school records, had nine O Levels, with high grades in mathematics. Apparently, he didn't attempt A Levels. As he had no idea what he wanted to do next, he was put to chartered accountancy in a London firm, Messrs Pridie, Brewster and Gold of Gray's Inn, because of a family connection. His Bedford housemaster, Mr Roseveare, had doubts about this. He had taken a small party of boys to the Fitzwilliam Museum in Cambridge in their last summer term and noted James's excitement at the paintings there, commenting afterwards to his wife, 'That boy will never be an accountant – he is an artist!' Thus the son of gifted creative parents embarked on a life in the City. He found it extremely stressful: mentally and physically constipating.

Soon he joined forces with a Garwood first cousin, Brooke Calverley, who was also in London studying to be an articled clerk, with equal lack of enthusiasm. At that time, James was living in a tiny hostel room with basin, hard narrow bed and single-bar gas fire, in the Belsize Avenue Residential Club. It was not far from Peggy Angus's London home, so she was able to come back into his life, as she had always hoped to do. Through her and her circle he began to rediscover his parents' friends, and to find out how his father was valued. In those spartan digs, at opposite ends of the table, the two boys toiled through columns of figures and books of law respectively, distracted by the din of carefree foreign students next door. Or amused themselves with impromptu comic scenes using the mimicry they were both so good at. Brooke describes them as 'two callow nineteen-year-old youths aching to be creative'. Both boys lived for the weekend when they could escape on Brooke's motorbike to Sussex to stay in primitive rusticity at Furlongs where, as Brooke records, Peggy 'happily sowed the seeds of artistic revolt in our tender minds'.

Life at Furlongs in 1958 had changed little since Eric and Tirzah first stayed there in the 1930s. There were the same iron bedsteads in little cottage rooms, the same oil lamps to be lit at dusk, the same garden privy swept by downland winds. Except that as the years passed, the walls had become covered with Peggy's vigorous hand-blocked wallpapers, and hung with paintings by her and her visitors; while woodwork, and even utensils, had been painted in her bright folk-art style. Dressed like a Russian peasant woman, usually in red, Peggy would dragoon the boys into useful tasks: house painting, digging the Elsan pit, or toting firewood and provender up to the dried-out dewpond on the downs for one of her celebrated bonfire parties. The rewards were fresh air, freedom from conventional restraints, and contact with the stream of creative people who always flowed through Peggy's door – among them some lovely

Furlongs, near Glynde, Sussex, 1970s
James Ravilious

arty girls. But James was still far too unsure of himself to do more than yearn for the bohemian life.

Peggy was an inveterate organiser, inclined to hector people in her forceful Scottish tones, but she had a wonderful gift for releasing creativity in the diffident. She had been teaching art for many years and fervently believed that art was for all, that everyone could, and should, express themselves creatively, given the right encouragement. She was also an ardent socialist. It horrified her that Eric and Tirzah's boy should be thrown into the very den of capitalism. 'Eric would turn in his grave,' she would say, 'If he had one.' Just as the strain of eighteen months of accountancy was beginning to affect James's health, the atmosphere at Furlongs, and Peggy's vehement left-wing opinions, got him drawing and changed his life.

On one of those escapes to Sussex in early 1959 he made two pencil sketches: one of Peggy's sitting-room, the other of the fine old wooden granary in the farmyard. Such strong and confident drawings they are that it is hard to believe that he had had no training, and that his teachers had not spotted any artistic talent in him since his mother's influence faded eight or more years before.

Now, all of a sudden, he found the nerve to make a complete change. He would abandon sums and the City, and try for art school. Hurriedly, he consulted artistic advisors. His parents' other friends were supportive. Edwin

Peggy Angus telling a creepy story,
Furlongs, Glynde, Sussex, 1984
James Ravilious

36

Smith and Olive Cook gave him suppers and encouragement, and Edward Bawden approved, in his dry way. James braved the understandable misgivings of the Swanzy family, and rushed in an application to St Martin's School of Art. He actually applied under an assumed name, hating the thought that Ravilious might gain him entry undeservedly. But his looks betrayed him. One of the members of the interviewing panel – I suspect it was Vivian Pitchforth, a contemporary of Eric at the Royal College – recognised the distinctive family features, and perhaps the drawing style too. But by that time James's portfolio had already secured him a place.

The sitting room at Furlongs, 1959 (pencil)
James Ravilious

3 . JAMES THE ARTIST

SO, IN THE AUTUMN OF 1959, James joined his brother John and Joanna Bawden in student digs in Artesian Road near Westbourne Grove, Bayswater, and began the artistic life in St Martin's dour building in Charing Cross Road. He was now twenty, perhaps slightly older than most of the other students, and initially more conventional in style, with a distinct air of City correctness in his haircut and clothes. A fellow student, Josephine Bayliss, remembers him looking more 'off-duty Sandhurst' than art student, in tweed jacket, grey flannels and a trilby hat. And he took his studies seriously, for he had a lot to prove. While others fooled around, he worked and thought hard. Josephine, and other contemporaries such as Marion Ogilvey, who worked on a nearby donkey in the life-drawing room, recall long philosophical discussions over coffee in the Lyons Corner House across the street. At this time, Tagore and de Chardin appeared on his one small bookshelf, as well as Gombrich and Berenson. Later there would be books by the Theosophist Krishnamurti, too.

The new life was a huge relief, but not without difficulties. Sex was still a crippling problem. He could have fun in a group, make people laugh, play sociable games, but a one-to-one relationship with a woman remained beyond his reach. The Sixties were getting going, but they didn't swing for James. He could only watch with envy as other male students casually worked their way through unending supplies of willing girls.

During this time there was also a family concern. It was James who had to cope initially when his brother John had a breakdown which would be diagnosed as schizophrenia. It was James who got him medical help, and James who was the only visitor he wanted to see in the grim surroundings of psychiatric hospital where he was treated for many months.

James's art school output was competent but not outstanding. His paintings show the struggle he had with paint; and with finding a style that was unlike his father's. This bothered him a lot. He learnt wood engraving from Clifford Webb, and could do lively designs in both wood and lino, but again he felt too much in his parents' shadow to be comfortable. However, St Martin's traditional training gave him two significant gifts. One was a reverence for the great artists of the past. Students were particularly encouraged to go to galleries and learn from the masters in all sorts of fields. Like Eric before him, James haunted the National Gallery, the Courtauld Collection and, above all, the V&A, where he spent many hours in the Print Room and among its mediaeval collections. The other gift was the all-important sense of form he developed under the guidance of teachers such as Vivian Pitchforth, by then very deaf and rather formidable, in the drawing studio at St Martin's. There, drawing was still seen as fundamental to an artistic training.

In his first summer vacation he made an unusual grand tour of Europe. Tyl Kennedy, an engineer and former schoolfriend of his brother John, had acquired an elderly car, a 1927 Swift. He invited James and Louisa Nicholson (daughter of the Modernist architect 'Kit' Nicholson and the textile designer 'E.Q.') to go with him in 'Matilda' all the way to Moscow and back. It was late July, 1960; the Iron Curtain had just lifted enough to allow western

tourists into the USSR, though few can have arrived by such an endearingly quaint method of transport. James took some undistinguished snaps, and kept notes of the outward trip, but as so often with holiday diaries his writing dried up when things got really interesting. In the first weeks it rained a good deal, apparently; they were often lost; and had to negotiate red tape, poor roads, food queues and primitive campsites. But helpful students assisted them, eager to practise their excellent English; and Matilda drew amused crowds wherever she parked. Lack of space obliged all three travellers to squeeze on to her small bench seat in front. Her fragile rear suspension collapsed just outside Kiev, needing several days for repair; but otherwise she carried them valiantly for some 8,000 miles. After a gruelling few days in Kiev while they had to get the car transported to a garage, find lodgings for themselves, try – unsuccessfully – to find adequate food (the boys went without for twenty-four hours,

Tyl Kennedy's 1927 Swift, 'Matilda', 1960 (pencil)
James Ravilious

according to James), taking wrong trolley buses or paying large sums for taxis for all the to-ing and fro-ing, James made this entry in his journal:

> Monday 22nd [August] Get up 7.30. Suddenly remember it's my 21st Birthday. Write diary. Others rather indignant at being woken at 8.45! Others not up so decide to go off on my own to see St Sophia and St Andrews if I could find them. Take a No 7 trolley & walk for about half an hour & to my amazement find myself at St Sophia's. Splendid gold domes & the most wonderful murals covering all the walls & roof inside. Many tourists. Some murals being rather hideously restored. Horrifying to see some hack student painting the figure of a saint when he obviously didn't feel anything about what he was doing.

It was a rather distinguished place to come of age: alone in the earliest Byzantine church in Russia, with great golden mosaics blazing down on him.

From Kiev they moved on to Kharkov and then Moscow. James wrote to Kay Swanzy from there: 'We have 9 days here before Leningrad. Weather has been awful last week but superb now. The people here are much happier thank goodness, Kharkov was the most miserable place I have ever visited, but fascinatingly so.'

They made a nervous departure at the Russian border. In a large gaunt building in the forest, stern-looking guards disappeared with their passports for a long time. But, once past the array of gun-emplacements, the opposite barrier was a single pole manned by a friendly young man; and there they were in Finland, and a startlingly different world. As James wrote home from the youth hostel in the old British sailing ship, *af Chapman*, in Stockholm harbour: 'Finland was a wonderful hospitable modern contrast to Russia, though not half so interesting – but everything *beautifully* colourful & well designed.'

It was during his time at St Martin's that James fell in love with France. John Swanzy's job with ICI subsidiary Lightning Zip Fasteners had moved him and Kay to a house backing on to the Seine at Poses, near Rouen. James often joined them for holidays there, and spent his time cycling alone to all the cathedrals and abbeys he could reach. He felt at home in France. He discovered by research through the Huguenot Society that Ravilious was probably an anglification of a Huguenot name (perhaps Ravelet originally, later Raveles) and he felt the call of his French blood. When things got him down in adult life the best tonic was always a few days in France.

The St Martin's era was on the whole a good time. He felt a sense of release, of life opening up, though he wasn't sure where it would take him, and there was still no real girlfriend in sight. When he left with his diploma he decided to get right away from London into retreat to try and find himself as an artist. Here Peggy Angus came to his aid once more. As well as renting Furlongs, she owned outright a traditional croft on the small Outer Hebridean island of Barra. It was rather grandly called Higgins House after a previous owner but, like most crofts, it was just a single low rectangle of rough stone walling with a tiny open fireplace at each end, although it had a noisy corrugated iron roof by then rather than the original thatch. Peggy had filled it with camp beds, rickety packing-case furniture, junk, artworks and *objets trouvés* from the shore. Two small windows looked out over a rocky slope of turf down to the machair – the fertile strip of land overgrown with turf and flowers just inside the dunes. Beyond them the Atlantic gleamed like beaten pewter all the way to Canada.

Higgins House was even more primitive than Furlongs: dark and draughty, and only warm if one sat close over the smoky little fire. It was lit by candles and paraffin, and had no telephone. Water came from a well, and basic food, much of it tinned, came by van twice a week. Anything else had to be fetched by bicycle from the one small 'town', Castlebay, four miles away around the coast along the only road. (In those days the superb seafood which

Higgins House, Barra, from above, 1972
James Ravilious

was plentiful round the island travelled in the opposite direction, to mainland city restaurants.)

Normally, Peggy spent some of her holidays at Higgins House, and lent it to friends for theirs. But now she was off on a long trip to study the folk art of Bali. She offered to lend the croft to James for a few weeks in exchange for some maintenance by way of rent. In the end he spent a whole year there, joined by Peggy and others intermittently. During that time he set to and completely lined the dilapidated tin roof – using timber reclaimed from an old church hall (all of which had to be lugged up over the rock-strewn turf) and created sliding wooden shutters for the roof-lights in the back slope operated on pulleys by ropes ingeniously counter-weighted by fishermen's floats

Peggy Angus by the fire, Higgins House, Barra, 1972
James Ravilious

filled with sand. He threw himself into the task, building as solidly as he could, and his work lasted for many years despite the damp and the constant battering it endured. The shutters are still in use today.

For a gregarious twenty-three-year-old it must have been rough and often solitary living, especially in the winter. The weather alone was a challenge. On Barra, although the Gulf Stream can bring halcyon days, the changeability is disconcerting. Hot sunshine can become fierce storm in a few short hours. Even in the April when we visited together ten years later, the crossing was horrendous, and the constant gale an exhausting companion. The noise of it never stopped, and if you ventured outside every loose hair on your head flogged your face till it was sore. It was strong enough to blow a Jeep over into a ditch. I don't know how James managed roofing work in those conditions. But clearly he enjoyed it. The confident independence of the island mentality appealed to him. The locals with their softly lilting voices made 'Hamish' welcome, and took him with them to ceilidhs in Castlebay from time to time, where a male dance partner was always popular as most of the sons of the island were working far from home. If people wondered why a healthy active young man spent so long 'doing nothing', James disarmed them. According to Peggy, he went to a fancy dress party in strange garb, with a large bone tied on his head – his title: 'Bone Idol'.

James was keen on birds, and Barra offered great northern divers, corncrakes, whooper swans and all sorts of sea-birds. On boat trips to uninhabited islands nearby there might even be a golden eagle or two. There were friendly seals, and fascinating trans-Atlantic flotsam on the shoreline to investigate. There might have been another diversion. I was half-sad to discover from a recent *Time Team* programme that the turf-covered mounds by the shore, which were exposed by a freak storm in 2005, form an important prehistoric site. James had loved 'arkieology' ever since prep school, and had worked on an Iron Age dig in Hampshire as a student. He would have been excited to know that he passed Bronze Age kists and a big Iron Age roundhouse every time he went down to collect driftwood for his fire.

It seems, however, that carpentry took precedence over art during his stay. Few paintings emerged from the Barra year. Two or three small oils on wood survive that give a good impression of the extraordinary simplicity of the landscape: olive-green, treeless hills sandwiched between grey sea and greyer sky. But it was an important rite of passage for James, and an extremely satisfying achievement which also paid a debt to Peggy. Eighteen years later she was still writing gratefully, 'Whenever I come back I bless you, James, for making Higgins liveable.'

Back in London the next year he found a part-time job at Hammersmith College of Further Education teaching O and A Level painting and drawing by day, and adult classes in the evenings. Teaching by example, he made some very nice gouache still-lifes at this time, and did a good deal of figure drawing.

He also lectured on the history of art, sharing his enthusiasms. He enjoyed teaching, and was clearly good at it. Later, I sometimes modelled for his figure drawing classes, so I was able to observe him at work. He didn't have authority in the disciplinary sense, but there was no doubting his seriousness about art, or his humanity. His pupils, some of them far from easy school drop-outs with drug problems, clearly felt he was on their side. One student, Wendy Morrison, wrote to me of her experience of doing O Level art with James. 'Jim brought out a sense of creativity in me that I would not have believed existed. The way I look at nature, shapes, colours, objects of all kinds, has a lot to do with the wonderful, sensitive teaching that I experienced in Jim's classes. He always made me see the positive in what I did, and although I got the O Level, what really mattered was the actual experience of working alongside other students in the most stimulating of classes.'

The part-time salary, combined with the last of his share of the Garwood money, allowed James to find a place of his own in the familiar Bayswater area, and to begin its transformation into a studio flat. By this time an understanding older woman had released him from the prison of virginity so he felt better about himself, but he was still unfocused as an artist.

At Hammersmith, his senior colleague in the art department, Elizabeth Clifford, became a friend. As a second string, she had a stall in Portobello Market. Her special interest was old photographs and photographic equip-

Still life with blue canister, c. 1968 (gouache)
James Ravilious

ment. She talked photography with James, and encouraged him to use a camera as a note-taking tool. It may have been at her suggestion that he went to see the Cartier-Bresson retrospective in March 1969, the first big photographic exhibition mounted by the V&A. This was a hugely significant moment in his life, for it opened his eyes to the artistic potential of photography beyond mere record: the power and resonance of '*le moment critique*'. Here, for the first time, he saw the swift-moving newsreel of life captured by an artist as *pictures*: pictures composed like paintings, although they might be made in the second when a running child's feet were off the ground; pictures that dwell in the memory. The revelation ignited an enthusiasm which would not burn out like the others. (This, incidentally, was the second V&A exhibi-

tion to influence the career of a Ravilious: it affected him as strongly as the Samuel Palmer one in 1926 had inspired his father.) The feel for design which James had inherited from Eric now came into play, as he began to look at life in terms of black-and-white patterns and forms. He rushed out and bought himself a decent camera. From this period come a touching portrait of one of his students, and a few photographs of street scenes around Hammersmith which clearly show the influence of Cartier-Bresson.

Portrait of a student, Hammersmith College
of Further Education, c. 1970
James Ravilious

4 . MY EARLY LIFE

LIKE JAMES, I too had lost my mother, a young actress called Jill Furse, but as a new baby, so I had no idea of her except from stage photographs, and from the tenderness which came into people's eyes and voices when they spoke of her. Their reminiscences told me that she was sensitive, loving and (in the old sense) gay, and that she was an actress of great promise, who played from the heart with touching honesty at a time when acting was still quite mannered. She had gone straight from stage school into London theatre success, and continued to find work there, though not always in very distinguished plays, acting with Vivien Leigh and Eric Portman, among others. Lilian Bayliss and Tyrone Guthrie wanted her to play Shakespeare's young heroines for them at the Old Vic, but war intervened. She played the second Mrs de Winter in the West End revival of the play of Daphne du Maurier's *Rebecca,* and had a small scene with Robert Donat in the original film of *Goodbye, Mr Chips.* The theatre director Norman Marshal wrote: 'I know that as a producer I shall never again meet an actress of her peculiar quality – that combination of exquisite beauty and ability to portray emotion with absolute purity and clarity.'

She and my father, Laurence Whistler, met in Wiltshire in 1937 through his brother Rex's friend Edith Olivier, who was a neighbour of Jill's grandfather, the poet Henry Newbolt. The Whistler boys had made much the same social journey as Eric Ravilious, rising from an undistinguished background by means of their talents (in their case with the help of a public school education partly funded, like James's, by more well-to-do relatives). Their mother was a country vicar's daughter who had married 'beneath her', much to her family's consternation; her choice a Hampshire builder. Neither was particularly educated or artistic.

Rex's precocious draughtsmanship took him to the Slade School of Art; Laurence's ability as a writer got him into Balliol College, Oxford. He was twenty-five when he met Jill and he fell in love at once. She was attracted, but

Jill and Laurence Whistler on honeymoon,
Berrynarbor, North Devon, 1939.
Celia Furse

wary for a while, and occupied with stage commitments. Their bond was poetry. He had won the first King's Gold Medal for poetry aged twenty-three, soon after leaving Oxford, but was now also reviving the long-lost art of point engraving on glass. They married on the eve of war in September, 1939.

But Jill's career was always in peril. She had an unrecognised auto-immune disease – probably a type of Lupus – which flared up at times of stress, cruelly cutting short some exciting roles. She also fell pregnant with my brother Simon later that year, which interrupted her acting for a while. Four years later, she was rehearsing for John Gielgud in his production of *The Last Rose of Summer* when she discovered I was on the way. That second pregnancy was one stress too many. In his account of their short time together, *The Initials in the Heart*, my father drew a moving portrait of a marriage that began as war broke out, flowered for a few idyllic months together until he was called up, and then survived on letters and brief meetings – 'lives', he called them – whenever he could get leave from army training camp; all of it intensified by the mood of war, and the possibility of his being killed. But in November 1944, in the cottage hospital at Torrington in North Devon where I had just been born, it was she who died, almost without warning. She was twenty-nine; Simon was four; and I was twelve days old.

Since my father was in the Army it now fell to my maternal grand-parents to take charge of me. Though they holidayed in Devon, they were based in London where my grandfather was Director of Recruitment in the Colonial Service. Because of the bombing they arranged to have me fostered in Devon for six months, while Simon, bereaved in a way I could not be, went to live in Oxford with his young aunt Theresa, Jill's much younger sister, who was soon to enter the University. We rejoined our grandparents later, in the care of my father's childhood nursemaid from Norfolk, Katy Buckle, who returned to look after us, and we lived with them first in London and then at Halsdon near the North Devon village of Dolton.

A small estate of manor house, woods and a few tenant farms, Halsdon had been in the Furse family for nearly three hundred years. It was a yeoman property, not at all aristocratic, which had gradually been added to by a line of country squires and clerics. The main house itself, though a magic place to children, is not beautiful or distinguished, the original cob farmhouse having been obscured by a sprawl of additions over the centuries, concluding with a heavy Victorian front. But its setting, in a saddle above the steep oak-furred sides of the sinuous River Torridge valley, has a remoteness and an air of romantic melancholy which has tugged at the heartstrings of generations of my family.

Buried in a wooded combe nearby was a cob-and-thatch cottage by a stream called Halsdon Mill, which had been the home of Halsdon estate workers and gardeners for at least two hundred years. It was very simple, very poetic. My mother was based there during the war, with Simon; and my father joined her for those precious 'lives' they had together. After she died, it remained a place of inspiration for him: he would go there alone to write. In my early years it was where Simon, Katy Buckle and I, and sometimes my grandmother, spent holidays from dingy war-worn London, immersed in the countryside, with a small black range to cook on, milk delivered in a can from the farm, and a tumbledown privy patrolled by spiders below the steep woods behind the cottage. Like the country children before us, we were bathed in front of the fire by candlelight, in an enamel hip-bath filled from smoke-blackened kettles on the stove, with a blanket on a clothes horse to shelter us from (some of) the draughts.

It has not been easy for anyone in my family to live up to the poetic intensity of my parents' love in the less highly charged relationships of normal life. It was particularly hard for Theresa, whom my father married when I was five, and who thus became my stepmother as well as my aunt. Twelve years younger than Jill, with fragile prettiness rather than beauty, Theresa was intellectual, a dreamer and very unconfident. She had felt outshone by her sister ever since early childhood; and although she got a first at Oxford (later publishing several distinguished books) and took on my father and us two children with the most loving intentions, she could never overcome the sense of being the 'second-best wife'. The fact that Jill remained his lifelong muse was insurmountable. The second marriage produced two more children, my half-siblings, Daniel and Frances, and was happy at times, especially in the early days, but it became increasingly strained by Theresa's long ups and downs of bipolar disorder which had a major impact on all our lives for the rest of hers. After many painful episodes the marriage broke down in 1978. My father moved to Wiltshire, and Theresa returned to North Devon.

When they married in 1950, I had, very reluctantly, to leave Halsdon for Lyme Regis, sixty miles away on the west Dorset coast, where we were all to live with my father's twice-widowed mother, Helen. I grew up at Lyme, an academic, introverted and nervous girl, attending the local co-ed grammar school, feeling nondescript, longing passionately to be as beautiful and talented as my mother, convinced that you had to be both to be lovable. It was only when I could get back to Halsdon for holidays that I could relax in self-forget-fulness. The secluded beauty of that countryside, the freedom to wander alone at all hours in the woods and river meadows, and the wildlife I encountered there, were my chief happiness in life. My brother Simon was my closest friend, but he was four years older, musical, and away at boarding school most of the time, so it was largely a case of hero-worship on my side, and kindly condescension on his, until the age gap levelled out later on.

Tense as it often was, family life at Lyme was not all unhappy in those early days. The town was a charming little seaside resort, and my grand-mother's house, Little Place, a small Regency villa with a large walled garden, a copse of tall trees and a view of Lyme Bay as far as the distant blue wedge of Portland Bill. But it was still too urban for me.

The house was something of a shrine to my artist uncle Rex whose death in Normandy had come a few months before my mother died. Gran spoke his name with loving reverence. His taste, his furniture and, above all, his works, surrounded us in every room. His personality, playful and romantic, seemed a benevolent spirit in the house. My father, who was six years younger and greatly in his debt artistically, devoted a large part of his time to curating his work, and writing about it. Since he shared Rex's love of Georgian style, we took that for the norm. (In any home of my father's the simplest label on a key, or box of nails, was written in elegant copperplate.) My young life, even more than James's, was therefore permeated by the legends of two gifted people, who meant so much to others, but whom I could never know.

When he was not writing poems, or working on books about my mother or Rex, my father was glass-engraving, a craft he had taught himself, and which he would gradually develop from a decorative skill for adorning commemorative gifts, in the rococo style shared with Rex, into an art capable of expressing his deep love of the Wessex landscape, and his beliefs about life and death. One of my best memories of that time is the sight and sound of him at work: Schubert playing softly in a darkened room; a goblet in my father's hands spot-lit on a black velvet tablecloth; and, just audible above the music, the faint ringing of the glass as he tapped it rapidly with a tungsten carbide point, building up a tiny sparkling scene in minute dots of light. He worked long hours, and when he was working we had to keep quiet. When he came off duty there were romps, silly games with the dog, elaborate literary jokes, poetry reading and picnics in the Dorset countryside that inspired him; but his work, his tastes and his opinions dominated family life, and we all submitted to them. For me as a child, his attention was a rare and special privilege which was always withdrawn too soon.

My half-siblings Daniel and Frances arrived when I was nine and twelve, respectively. I learnt a good deal of parenting from helping to look after them – willingly on the whole, though it is hard to believe now that as a child of twelve I was sent on a railway journey, with changes, in sole charge of a feisty little three-year-old brother. I was considered usefully 'sensible' and 'capable' in those days. No one knew how much responsibility frightened me.

Winning an Oxford scholarship was a boost to my confidence, but women students had to work hard to justify their places then, and I was haunted by a sense of guilt if I didn't, so I never made the kind of explorations that I should have done. A little acting, and a lot of serious-minded talk, were my main achievements – apart from a degree in English. Living in such a beautiful city was the happiest part of it.

Afterwards, preferring the arts world to the academic, I bought time with a secretarial training and a post as Principal's Secretary at Newnham College, Cambridge, for a couple of years. In 1969, when I met James, I was in London to look for a more fulfilling job – but still without confidence, or any clear sense of direction.

We pooled our hidden loneliness and made the closest friendship either of us had ever had.

5 . TOGETHER

SOON ALL MY FREE TIME was spent in James's modernist studio flat near Westbourne Grove. It was startlingly unlike any Whistler interior. The last of his share of the family money in trust had enabled James to spend £4,000 on the lease of the top two floors of a four-storey Victorian terrace house on the north side of Talbot Road, number 64. Letting the lower level as two bedsits, he had put in a bathroom and a new staircase and, with his own hands and help from a friend, removed inner walls, ceilings and a chimney full of ancient soot in order to convert the four small rooms at the top into a single space. The ceiling was now supported by a square central pillar, with living quarters on the south side and studio on the north. James, armed with books such as *Teach Yourself Electricity in the House*, did most of the rebuilding, re-flooring and re-wiring himself, with painstaking care, and very little professional help.

He was keen on Le Corbusier at the time, so the space was very simple, pale and full of light. Wherever possible, the measurements obeyed the Golden Section principle of ideal proportions. The furniture, which he made himself, was functional, sturdy, and white or pale grey. A few rectangles of brilliant primary colours punctuated the white: one scarlet and one cobalt blanket on the home-made king-size bed; chrome yellow cushions on the white-covered settee; a chrome-painted stool, and a cobalt one, and foursquare Habitat mugs in scarlet, yellow or blue. Everything else was in stainless steel. One little flourish was a square metal light over the table suspended with an invisible counterweight so that it stayed put when you moved it up or down. His nephew Tom Ullmann remembers the mystery of this when he was small, and how James would call up to 'a little man in the ceiling' to haul and hold it up.

The modernism ended there, however, for James was no minimalist. He despised housework and actively disliked tidiness. So the worktop was usually scattered with washing-up, sawdust and little bits of electrics; the light-grey flooring grubby; and the studio piled high with carpentry tools, golf clubs, a bicycle, a quarter-size snooker table and junk, as well as his painting things.

But it was a delightful living space: both positive, and, once you had gasped your way up five steep flights of stairs, relaxing. Two big round-topped windows looked south on to an area that was rundown and full of life. From those windows one could watch, almost at eye level, majestic planes sailing in towards Heathrow Airport through the pearly London cloud. Below, one could observe the punters' cars nosing along the curb to choose one of the teenaged street girls shivering in cardigans and ankle socks. I can still hear the familiar sound-track of that life: the slow castanets of a totter's horse, and the mournful two-note chant of 'Rag-bone', mingling with an ice cream vendor's saccharine tune; the wow and throb – Jimi Hendrix-style – of electric guitars in the dingy terraces at the back; shrill arguments in basements; rich West Indian laughter bursting from street corner groups; and the blare of police cars racing to sort out the students opposite, who got drunk or stoned and created scenes in the small hours. We had a ringside seat, and it was all quite distracting.

In those days, James was not difficult to distract. Between the part-time hours teaching art at Hammersmith College, he was still trying to be a painter, but he could not settle to a style. He was in a Cézanne phase when I first knew him, struggling with imagined landscapes that never quite came right. He loved the texture of thick oil paint, but couldn't handle it to his satisfaction. I had not seen a painter at work before. I was puzzled to see him stare at a canvas for hours, add one daub, stare some more . . . and then scrape it off again. This happened a lot, and the results looked rather tortured to me. Later he abandoned that for the pure abstract of Mondrian's *Compositions* series. At first he actually painted his carefully composed rectangles and grids in primary colours and black, using masking tape for an accurate straight edge. But they had to be laboriously repainted so many times he hit on an easier solution. He bought electrician's plastic tape in the same bright colours and cut it with great care into the necessary strips and little squares with a blade. These were easier to reposition. I had come from a family to whom figurative was the only art. Abstract was a closed book to me. James explained it as he worked.

When painting got him down, as it frequently did, he would suddenly suggest a diversion. It might be, 'Let's go and watch planes!' We would dig out John Fletcher, a friend from art school who owned a van, and rattle down to Heathrow for the day. In those pre-terrorism times you could get away with parking by the perimeter fence almost underneath the flight path as gleaming leviathans took off over your head, their roar vibrating your guts like jelly. Jumbo jets were the novelty then, and soon Concorde herself. Other trips took us to the Clapham Transport Museum, the Museum of Childhood at Bethnal Green, or on the No. 31 bus to old haunts of James's at Chalk Farm and Primrose Hill. Once we went to Elstree for a half-hour flight in a four-seater Piper Cherokee training plane, just for the hell of it. Then there were the gallery visits – to specific exhibitions, such as *Treasures of Tutankhamun* – or simply to refresh James's memory of individual favourite works, and to share them with me. On Saturdays we sauntered through the market in Portobello Road, which ran across the far end of our street, and watched avant-garde films on the tiny screen of the Edwardian Electric Cinema there. Coming up to London as a nervous country girl I had always thought it an ugly and alarming place. James clearly felt at home there, and I learned to find it exciting in his company.

Another diversion was snooker on the table in the studio. James had inherited his parents' love of the game, and he and various male friends would play late into the night fortified with endless mugs of sweet tea.

His relish of technology, and breaking news, were major distractions all his life, for when he had an enthusiasm on the go he was completely gripped. He would wake up talking of it; return to it at intervals all through the day; ring up friends to discuss it; and even plunge in with surprised fellow travellers on trains. In the summer of 1969 he was all fired up about the mission to the moon. He collected a great sheaf of press coverage, and that July, when Apollo 11 landed, we stayed awake all night listening to radio news. James was thrilled by its success, and by the sense of history being made. The following year we queued for hours at the Science Museum to file past some of Buzz Aldrin's 'fine sandy particles': a tiny heap of khaki-coloured powder that was Moon Dust.

His father Eric had been nicknamed 'The Boy' by his friends. It would have suited James just as well. Looking back I'm amused to see how meekly I followed him in pursuit of these boyish delights, much as I had trailed after Simon when I was the admiring little sister in his wake.

A few weeks after we got together I took a holiday before starting my new secretarial job which was at the National Council for Voluntary Organisations, in a department co-ordinating local history groups and amateur drama societies nationwide. I went down to Devon to stay with my grandparents at Halsdon for a week. There I made James a scruffy little sketch of the Torridge valley looking northwest towards Torrington – executed in the drizzle, with writing ink on notepaper for want of proper materials. 'Enclosed is a scrawl,'

I wrote 'of my favourite view – at dusk on a wet evening. I was born in the shadow of that spire.' This sketch was his introduction to the countryside he would make his own. He would photograph that very view again and again.

It was during this short break that we wrote our only letters to each other, for we were never apart again for more than a few days, except for one three-week trip to France when he was too busy to write. So a handful of short, often jokey, notes is all there is in writing of our thirty years together.

The day after I left London he wrote: 'Hello! My beautiful, so special, darling girl – I cannot forget you for one minute so *really* you always seem to

View across the River Torridge,
Halsdon, Dolton, 1969 (pen and wash)
Robin Ravilious

be here – I feel everything in a new & subtle light or a quiet sound – & I am in great danger of trying to write poetry to you so here is my message in honest Canaveral (Huston) 09.01 hrs – status check – / Destination Whistler Robin – / crew status – nuts – / inboard computer status – nuts/.' (All his life James would backtrack from emotion to humour like this. He found it difficult to express deep feelings and almost always retreated from them into a joke.) 'I'm so happily madly jumpy,' he added, illustrating the fact with crazy doodlings.

From Devon I planned to move on to my actual home at Lyme Regis to see my family. But James was getting impatient. 'Dream up some lovely mystifying way that we could meet – or should I? You know the land – every day now is a day without you – make it soon.' I would have to change trains in Exeter, so his solution was to come all that way on a day return ticket just so that we could spend a couple of hours together. It was his first actual sight of Devon. We met on the platform, and walked up to the city centre talking hard. On a busy pavement in Queen Street I mentioned how happy I was, whereupon he dropped my suitcase, literally, to take me in his arms. I showed him the cathedral and he bought me some Victorian earrings. Then we travelled as far as Axminster together. A few days later he made another trip, to Salisbury, to meet me for the day. We visited the cathedral, then picnicked in steamy sunshine on a bank of the River Avon. Again, James was eager, amorous and talkative. I thought these trips crazily extravagant – but I was longing to see him too. After Exeter I wrote:

Hello and thank you – thank you for a lovely day. I haven't written before either 'cos it was so nice I couldn't think how to say so – and anyway it didn't seem to need saying . . . I have found a new word to describe you: FEBRILE. Perhaps you don't think it's very complimentary – but actually it describes one of the things I like best about you. For some curious reason, I have been stuck for some time with men who weren't at all febrile so that, emotionally & 'sensitively', I always felt as if I were dancing round & tugging at my lead waiting for them to catch up. But with you I have to run, & dodge about like a hare, to keep up. Very enjoyable & salubrious exercise. I feel tense, and light, and quick-silvery . . .

While I was at Lyme James went down to Sussex to stay with Peggy at Furlongs. He wrote from there:

I'm looking across a warm rustling wheat field coming high up to the window and a dove is cooing just what I wanted to say to you. The farmer is grumbling downstairs – now laughing – & there's a flea on my ankle. This is the first hour of the harvest, & no sheaves but sacks & bales. I will do some lifting soon, if my back will take it, though it's finger nails that go. . . . I am tired & febrile after a night spying on the universe & the waning moon through the telescope. Unfortunately best seen at 3 am this morning! . . . I am so full of hope & of seeing you soon I hardly dare to expect it – to be so wonderful again & again.

After a day's harvesting he turned to painting, partly to avoid the crowd of eighteen visitors that Peggy had accrued. 'I feel rather like doing landscapes as the Elizabethans might & even put lots of people in too, surrounded by weeds & flowers & corn with poppies. I like doing small paintings . . .' He concluded with a little watercolour of the view from his bedroom window (one that his father had painted, too). 'Here is the view,' he wrote. 'I've made it rather pritty-pritty but it gives you an idea. Now I shall walk down the middle of this landscape & post it. With lots of love – your Jim.'

He mentions casually that his back is not up to much lifting in the harvest field. He had been having mild backache for a while. He blamed it on an over-energetic game of table tennis. On his return to London he went to his doctor expecting a soothing liniment. She asked some surprising questions, organised tests, and referred him to a specialist at St Mary's Hospital, Pad-

Here is the view —.

dington. By the time I got back clouds were gathering, and faces looking grave. Over the next weeks there were blood tests and a biopsy, then a horrible angiogram (the injection of blue dye into his whole body via the veins in his feet) and finally the clouds acquired a name. It was Hodgkin's Lymphoma – then a relatively difficult-to-diagnose cancer of the lymphatic system – and he had a tumour in a lymph node near his spine.

The ritual of tests and the stomach-churning wait for their results, which would soon become a way of life, was new to us then. So was the oh-so-English understatement of medical talk. What exactly did 'It could be nasty' mean? James played the gentlemanly game, flinching from anything as embarrassing as direct enquiry about his prognosis. He kept up his normal cheerful front, putting everyone else at their ease. He even lent a sympathetic ear, late

View from Furlongs window, 1969 (watercolour)
James Ravilious

one night on the ward, to a trainee doctor's fears that he, too, had the same disease. But I found the dark cloud of unknowing too hard to bear. I went privately to the medical bookshop in Praed Street and waded through an enormous encyclopaedia of disease. After page upon page of all the variants of lymphoma, their indications, diagnoses, palliative treatments and so on, the concluding comment was all too brief: 'Invariably fatal.' I kept it to myself.

Mercifully, the book was behind the times. James's specialist, Dr Hulbert, and his team were doing pioneering work with cobalt radiotherapy to zap this aggressive type of lymphoma. The double good fortune of having an alert GP, and being in the St Mary's Hospital catchment area, postponed that sentence for thirty years.

At this point, apart from Simon, who lived near us, my family had not met James, or heard much about him. Now I had to announce not only that I had met Mr Right, but that he was dangerously ill. I wrote to my father and Theresa:

> Anyway, you will have gathered that I love him very, very much – he is all that I ever vaguely dreamed of, and a real person on top of that! We are very close, and growing together all the time, which is so lovely. In fact, in a lot of ways, I spose we are very alike. . . . So life is rather harrowing at the moment, half-exquisite, half-heartbreaking – and no clear future at all. He is obviously badly ill – or potentially so – but the doctors are so brutally cagey. All the scraps we have to go on are: 'It's pretty serious – but no immediate urgency' . . . and 'Don't make any plans for the future yet.' Obviously they are absolutely the top specialists in Britain for this particular disease – & they can't say anything definite till they see how the treatment goes. This started yesterday – & seems not to be too unpleasant. It means he will have to be in and out of the hospital for the next 8 weeks in the first instance, & then – heaven knows.
>
> Meanwhile, he is being marvellous about it – tho' we both get terrible spasms sometimes, & silly little things give one sudden nightmares – probably

quite unfounded. He manages to get the maximum out of hospital life, making friends, doing odd jobs, & taking a real scientific interest in what they are doing to him. And when he's let out we have gay times & do things together in the social/sightseeing line according to his strength.

One wouldn't really think him ill at all, except that he's easily tired, & rather subdued – for him. . . . The great thing is to be together as much as possible – & to have things out in the open – however terrifying – which we do, and then to put them aside and get on with ordinary life, which we also do as far as possible.

Indeed, we are becoming a byword in his (very nice) ward for fooling, & for generally treating the place like a hotel (out for the weekend, or a concert, sauntering in at breakfast time, or 10.00 pm) . . .

Once the treatments began things were not quite as bad as we feared. The rays were focused on a small patch of his back which made it sore. He was generally tired, but able to lead a reasonably normal life, though it was increasingly punctuated by sudden flu-like exhaustion. He even carried on part-time teaching at Hammersmith for a while, and we made short trips here and there. The treatment (or perhaps the illness itself) affected his body thermostat. He would always be sensitive to cold thereafter. And in the short term, it reduced his immunity to other diseases. He had an alarming bout of pleurisy a few months later. However, the doctors were encouraging. At the end of the course of treatment they said he would have to have regular checks for the rest of his life, but that if the lymphoma did not return within two years the future would look 'quite promising'.

All in all, 1969 was quite a year for James. He had discovered a passion for photography, met his future wife, and been diagnosed with cancer – in the space of six or seven months. All three factors were to concentrate his mind.

6 . REPRIEVE

AS HE BEGAN TO RECOVER his strength, we travelled about introducing each other to our respective families and friends. I had already met his step-father Henry Swanzy, warmly concerned at James's hospital bedside (and reminded of Tirzah's last years, no doubt). Now we visited James's former guardians, John and Kay Swanzy, who were friendly, my Oxford credentials having earned some kudos. I'm not sure they had ever expected much of James, but I know they were fond of him. (John would become proud of him later on.) We had lunch in a Bloomsbury café with a trio of Tirzah's sisters, perched in a row like elegant and vociferous swallows. James's sister Anne came up from Birmingham with her violinist husband Louis Ullmann and their three children, Tom, Sarah and Martha. If I felt under inspection, it was only for a moment as they were as open and friendly as James. Anne has her mother's warm straightforwardness.

My brother Simon (by now a professional viola player and glass engraver) got on well with James from the start. They had similarly boyish enthusiasms and humour. When he was a little stronger, I took James to Lyme

Regis, where his artistic background was approved – my father had long admired Eric's work (hence those Wedgwood plates on our shelves) – though James's jokiness didn't quite come up to the sophisticated literary standards of my father's wit.

We also went to Halsdon where my elderly Furse grandparents were being looked after by my uncle Nic and his wife Jane. James fitted in well there, too, and indeed looked rather like a Furse. I showed him the sights of Halsdon: its views, its woods, the river's wide meadows and pools. Then, as we walked to the village one morning, I casually pointed out Addisford, the tiny cottage over a stream which Grandfather had given me in my teens. With its thatched roof, four little windows, and central rustic porch, it was like a child's drawing of a house then – small and humble, with an endearingly naive

Addisford Cottage near Dolton,
before renovation, 1970
James Ravilious

expression. It was rented out at that time, and my ownership still had a rather dream-like quality. It didn't seem very probable that it could actually belong to me; and certainly I saw no prospect of ever living there. I knew that Grand-father had given it to me, as he had given Halsdon Mill to Simon, because he understood how deeply we loved Halsdon, and wanted to secure us each a piece of it, whatever happened in the future to the main estate. It was also, in his eyes, the share we would have had from our mother if she had lived.

Early in that dark autumn I had moved in officially with James. By the following spring, 1970, we were so much a couple that we slid imperceptibly into wedding plans. There was no decisive moment. It would have embarrassed James to propose in the conventional way. And, anyway, we were already beyond anything so formal. But somehow arrangements began for us to marry – in London (so as not to bother my family too much) at the little Georgian church of St Giles-in-the-Fields, Holborn, on 1 September that year. Though I could not honestly claim to be 'a spinster of this parish', rules were bent for us because I worked nearby in Bedford Square, and occasionally went to lunchtime services. We made all the arrangements ourselves, as cheaply as possible. James cut a little wood engraving for the hand-written and photo-copied invitation. I hand-sewed my very simple dress, to which Theresa added a wreath of Dorset corn and a posy of small red roses and corn on the day. We were married by the immensely tall and charismatic Bishop of Maidstone, Geoffrey Tiarks, who had been our vicar at Lyme. Lovely Baroque music in keeping with the church interior was provided by Simon and three friends who at that time made up the Georgian Quartet. Simon also took the only photo-graphs. The pub across the road laid on a far-from-sumptuous wedding break-fast of plonk and curling sandwiches in a narrow covered balcony like the wheelhouse of a ship. Here we all drank from my father's wedding gift: a glass goblet engraved with our names and the date around a sheaf of corn.

I had found the organising of such a big event a considerable strain, so

James and Robin after their wedding, London, 1970
Simon Whistler

I was more anxious than happy till it was all over. But in fact things went extremely well, mainly because the Ravilious and Whistler clans had so many similar or overlapping connections that they were all delighted to meet each other and to celebrate the link that we were making. One of James's uncles looked me over benignly as we greeted him at the door and simply said, 'Good show!' The guest I was happiest to see was my beloved Katy Buckle, who had been my mother-substitute when I was small. Now seventy, she had made the long journey from her Norfolk village. I gave her my posy, which she took home and preserved, growing a succession of corn rows from it for years. She used to send us a few ears of it each year on our anniversary.

The following day we set off by train to Vienna. We stayed on the outskirts in a village guesthouse just below vineyards and wooded hills, and began to relax. We ate well, drank local wine out of earthenware beer mugs, and spent our days looking at pictures. Neither of us had expected the wealth of Brueghel, Giorgione, Rembrandt and Velázquez in the Kunsthistorisches Museum, nor the wonderful drawings in the Albertina. James bought prints above our budget of an Appenine landscape sketch by Claude Lorrain and a tumbledown yard by Rembrandt, both of which would inspire him later on. From Vienna he wrote to thank my father and Theresa for their part in the wedding. 'Thank you also for delivering Robin so beautifully adorned which also I shall never forget. . . . Tomorrow we are off to Salzburg . . . and then on to Venice – having seen the Venetian painting in Vienna my chops drool to see what Venice has in store. It also makes me long to get down to work again . . . We are now off again to stuff ourselves silly – life is very good.'

Life went on being good in the next couple of years. James's health checks were positive, his energy levels recovering. He resumed his teaching at Hammersmith, and took on a few hours at Westminster School as well. We socialised, and visited Furlongs and Barra. I did evening courses at the City Literary Institute, and began to work part-time for Peggy Angus on her eccentric, and doomed, attempt to revive Celtic art in the Hebrides. We saw Peter Brooke's unforgettable version of *A Midsummer Night's Dream*. James was not as interested in theatre as I was, but he was bowled over by that production. We also signed on with a charity called Task Force which organised volunteers to make regular visits to the vulnerable and lonely in the Paddington area. James befriended a dear old man, Fred Millar, who had been Lord Rothschild's coachman before the First World War. Like many of our 'clients' he was entirely alone in the world.

Now James even had the energy to return to furniture making from time to time, building a sturdy dining table in solid ash for one lot of friends, a chessboard table for another, a kitchen dresser as a wedding present for Simon and his new wife Jenni and, for me, a five-drawer lockable bureau which he took the trouble to veneer with thin ply, even though it was to be painted white. He inlaid the folding desk top with part of the pale grey lino left over from the floor. The piece was elegantly proportioned as always, and quietly modern, with the bent stainless steel handles he always favoured. The Ravilious craftsman streak was strong in James: he always bought the best tools for any job, whether he could afford them or not, and carried out the work with painstaking precision.

In those days he also had time to create home-made Christmas cards for friends and family each year. Sometimes it was a wood engraving, sometimes a lino-cut. The most elaborate one, *The Twelve Days of Christmas*, was a combination involving a 6" × 7" master in wood-engraving, and three separate lino-cuts to overlay it with colours. It consisted of twelve lively little vignettes in which traditional holy scenes mingled with modern ones. I rather doubt if angels and helicopters had ever featured in the same artwork before.

When he was at work I began timidly to draw again. I had always dabbled in drawing – chiefly lady-like watercolours of flowers – but I felt extremely tentative about it. In O level art at school I had earned high marks,

having the knack of copying accurately the outline of still lifes: the obligatory loaf of bread or pair of shoes that were set in those days. I would add a bit of shading, but my drawings were limp and two-dimensional. They had meant nothing much at home, where linear standards were so much higher. With university in mind I had been steered towards more academic subjects for A level. Now James the teacher could not resist taking my drawing in hand. He pounced at once on my lack of form – to him the absolute essential, the

Twelve Days of Christmas, 1971
(wood engraving and three lino-cuts)
James Ravilious

sine qua non, of all graphic art. He always judged severely even the most distinguished artists, including his father, by that primary criterion. But it was not a concept that anyone had ever put to me before, and it took some learning. To begin with I had to grasp what he wanted. '*Feel* the shape as you draw,' he would say, making exaggerated stroking movements in the air. 'Pull this forward. Push that back.' He would make me stand back at a distance to see my drawing clearly as a whole (an important lesson for someone used to working meticulously at close quarters); and he would tell me to turn my paper upside down to assess the solidity of the shapes without the distraction of what they represented. He also made me look at the spaces *between* things, and their importance. It took me a while to interpret his orders with the pencil in my hand, but I caught on gradually. I don't think he ever looked at a piece of my work without at once pointing out any weakness of form. It was the way to learn, of course, but sometimes painful none the less. His praise was rare, but precious.

Being literal-minded about artwork, I sometimes thought to myself, rebelliously, that his own drawings, apart from some of his portrait sketches, were so preoccupied with form that they conveyed little specific detail. But there was no doubting his authority, his inner certainty, on the subject of drawing, and that was something I respected – the main thing I respected in those days when, to be honest, he seemed such a dilettante otherwise. Much as I loved his impulsive enthusiasm, I did wonder if he would ever find himself a clear direction.

This private concern, coupled with my own lack of plan, made our next move a worry, for a new shadow had loomed ahead. In 1972 we were going to be turned out of the flat. Our section of the north side of Talbot Road was to be redeveloped, and we faced a compulsory purchase order, the proceeds of which were not enough to get us anything similar in inner London. James's solution was simple: we would go and live at Addisford.

It seems rather extraordinary now that moving to my much-loved countryside was his idea, not mine; and that he embraced it excitedly, while I dragged my feet. But to me it was an alarming step. For two people to move to the back of beyond without any paid work in prospect was a risk. When one of them was in remission from cancer it was, to my mind, foolhardy – though I didn't want to say so. At Addisford we would be seven rural miles from a doctor; twenty from a hospital; and neither of us could drive. On the other hand, it was a beautiful and inspiring place; and it was ours. There would be no mortgage to glower over us; no rent to pay; and my grandfather would be delighted that his gift had been justified. How well justified, alas, he would never know, though he did live to see us installed, and James's photographic work begun. I suppressed my fears and gave in somewhat tearfully.

The plan came together gradually. To begin with, there was much to be thought about to improve the cottage – a project James relished – using the compensation money. At that time, Addisford was almost completely unmodernised. Downstairs, between the bulbous three-foot thick cob walls, it had one small living room and a narrow larder. Up the irregular twisting stairs there was just one large bedroom, with a perilously sagging ceiling, partitioned off with planks to make a second room not much wider than a single bed. There was a water tap in the lane, a small Rayburn stove in the living room, and a lean-to lavatory with plank seat and bucket at one end of the house, accessible only from outside. There was also another lean-to, on the other end, which contained the old copper in which the weekly Halsdon laundry used to be done in my childhood. There was no electricity or telephone. The garden, once the pride of Reg Baker, my grandparents' gardener, had reverted to rough damp meadow and groves of hogweed six feet high. Set in a typical Devon combe, the cottage came with a five-acre sloping pasture up behind, a bit of steep mixed woodland known as Rushleigh Copse, full of bluebells and wild cherry trees, to the right; and a soggy patch of alders to the left. The front boundary was Rushleigh Brook, a small rocky stream through which one had to drive, further up, to reach the lane to the cottage; or else cross on foot by a plank bridge. The village was nearly a mile away up steep, narrow West Lane.

We made several trips to Devon to camp in the empty cottage. Sometimes James's architect friend Tim Nicholson (brother of Louisa who had gone on the Russian trip) came too, to design the modernisation we needed. In the August of 1971, we stayed up the road at Halsdon Mill, at first with Simon and Jenni, and then alone there, while we worked on Addisford. It was an idyllic time. By now James's doctors were cautiously optimistic, and he was full of the joys of escape from deadly illness, and of new beginnings. I wrote home an account of it all:

> He by the way is now more in love with Addisford & the country life than I am, I think, & deep in plans towards moving here soon. He is serene and healthy and undistracted and we've been happier here these last few days alone together than I think we have ever been – so it all seems to point one way . . . Meanwhile, 'playing houses' has included the slashing of nettles, the cutting of trees, the replastering of walls, repainting of same & woodwork of windows, the sweeping of the chimney & the ceremonial First Lighting of the Fire (yesterday). Also the purchasing of 2 dear little bunk beds which we hope to christen shortly, plus the making of basic furniture, and the acquiring of neighbours round about. In between all this we have bicycled (exhaustingly) round the countryside (17 miles one day! I'm a 3-day cripple after that sort of thing and have to get-off-and-push over molehills but he goes pedalling on). Or he has bird-watched exhaustively in the grounds . . . Tonight, however, James, in the very best cottager tradition, is making a bench – in the kitchen by lamplight – for his bride. (Actually, it's a plank ingeniously supported by the sawn-off bed heads from the old Wellington beds!)

As well as enthusiastic nest-building James wandered about recording Halsdon and its surroundings, taking photos of my grandparents and of the locals I introduced him to, as a record for the family. Most were just snaps, not very good technically as yet, but among them were portraits that have become increasingly precious with time.

There were pictures of Jean Pickard, for instance, one of our nearest neighbours, who meant a lot to me. She was not a Devonian, but a tall dark Scot from a farming family in Ayrshire. She had come to Dolton as a children's nanny. She married Doltonian Frank Pickard, her employer's driver, and together they farmed at Woolridge, one of the Halsdon farms. She was handsome, intelligent, warm-hearted and tough enough to run the farm alone while Frank was away in the war. Even on her own like this, she had yielded to my grandmother's persuasion and taken me on – a motherless new baby – as well. I spent the first eight months of my life at Woolridge lying in my pram in the hedge while lambing, haymaking and harvest went on around me.

Jean Pickard at her gate, Woolridge, Dolton, 1972
James Ravilious

7 . A NEW PERSPECTIVE

THE COMPULSORY PURCHASE of the Talbot Road flat would come into force in the autumn of 1972, so finding work in Devon became a priority. We researched schools and colleges where James might teach, and one morning in London he wrote to the Beaford Centre, an arts organisation we had heard about in a village two miles north of Dolton. It had been established six years earlier by the Dartington Hall Trust. James offered himself as a teacher of drawing or wood engraving. The director, John Lane, invited him for interview when we were next down.

On the appointed day James set off for Beaford on his bicycle. He was gone for hours. The interview turned into a long and enthusiastic talk about art and artists, and the start of a lifelong friendship. James found the intellectual level of John's conversation daunting, for he himself was not an intellectual, and well aware of it. His approach to art was instinctive and sensuous; and John's highbrow style could be quite challenging. But they had a lot to share because they loved so many of the same artists, from Duccio to Thomas Bewick. It also emerged that John's wife Truda had once taught art under Peggy

Angus in a London school. James very much admired Truda's delicate, spiritual drawings. It was immensely encouraging to him to find such cultivated people in the next village – people for whom the arts were a central part of life, as they were for him. John offered him an evening class teaching wood engraving, which he took for a few terms. Also, he told him about a project of his: the Beaford Archive.

Arriving as founding director of the Beaford Centre in 1966, John had discovered an intimate, quietly beautiful piece of countryside that was still to a large extent insulated, by geography and local temperament, from the modern world. Mechanisation had certainly begun to arrive during, or soon after, the Second World War, but much of the land was poor for commercial farming – wet and hilly, with cold soil in steep rushy little fields defined by enormous hedgebanks – and few of the small farmers who worked it had much cash or enthusiasm for modernising. They carried on in their few acres much as their parents had done, with a mix of cattle, sheep and arable, but with less and less help as they got older and their children moved away. They were in any case a self-reliant breed, rooted in their native land, and often unwilling to look beyond it, or to believe that innovation could improve on the traditional lore they had learned at their father's knee. In many ways they were the end of a line running

John Lane at the Beaford Centre, 1974
James Ravilious/Beaford Archive

back to the Anglo-Saxon settlers of the early eighth century; and indeed some of them had Saxon surnames which could be traced to farmsteads only a few miles away from where they were now living, a testament to their settledness. The poet Ted Hughes, who farmed there in the 1960s, described them in the preface to his *Moortown Diary*: 'The farmers lived lightly in the day and the year, but heavily in that long backward perspective of their ancient landscape and their homes. The breed was so distinct, so individualised and all of a piece, they seemed to me almost a separate race.'[2]

Because there was so little capital – few of them could have dreamed of borrowing from the bank – and no particular reason for outside traffic to divert from the main road up from Exeter to the north coast, the district remained a backwater. This meant buildings and villages were not so quickly modernised as elsewhere; and communities were still networks of mainly local people.

John Lane, inspired by writers such as H. J. Massingham and George Ewart Evans, and artists such as Tom Hennell, recorders of rural England in the 1930s and '40s, saw that this old-fashioned style of life, 'of precarious fragility', as he put it, enshrined traditions going back centuries, traditions that had once been common all over England, but which by then were fading in most other parts of the country. He knew it wouldn't resist the modern world much longer, and felt it an important part of the Beaford Centre's work to photograph it quickly before it disappeared. By a wonderful coincidence, when James turned up, the first photographer engaged to do this, Roger Deakins (now a distinguished cinematographer), had just moved on, so John was looking to replace him. John would later write of the project: 'I didn't want pale documentation at all; or an avant garde approach out of step with the culture of the area. I was looking for . . . someone capable of showing North Devon people to themselves.'

Though James demurred that he was quite untrained as a photographer, John invited him to take 'a few photos' anyway, saying that it didn't really matter what the quality was like, as long as the record was made. That meeting changed James's life.

He was nervous, but extremely excited by the commission, thinking, planning, talking about it all day long. It was a natural progression from the family record he had just been making, and it appealed to the deep-seated instinct he had, like his father and many other artists ever since the eighteenth century, to capture, to pin down, the essence of a loved but vulnerable piece of England.

The move from London was a challenge: our king-size bed and enormous plan chest (both made by James) had to be got down five flights of stairs at one end of the trip, and carried all the way up the lane at the other, as the big removal van could not get further than the ford. But we enjoyed the journey as the friendly removal men invited us to ride down in state with them in their cab. We just managed to shoehorn everything into the cottage, but it was overcrowded, even then.

As soon as we had moved in, we were off again on a holiday to Greece with my father and Theresa, where we found ourselves more interested in Greek village life, and the almost mediaeval farming of the northern uplands, than the classical sites that inspired my father, which seemed to us too crowded and commercialised to have kept their magic. However, the holiday taught James a valuable, if painful, lesson. He had just bought himself a light meter, and either it was faulty or he set it wrong. Enthusiastically, he posted back reels of film to be processed ready for our return. But when we got home he discovered that every single negative he had taken was too dark. He would always service and double-check his equipment carefully after that.

Once we were home the new life began in earnest. Two things were urgently needed: better transport, and a darkroom so that James could do his own processing. He solved the transport problem by buying a scooter. It was only just adequate for the steep hills of North Devon, and very slow. But it had the advantage of being cheap, and easy to 'lose' if he spotted a potential subject and needed to park out of sight in a hurry. He had something of a Monsieur Hulot air when he rode it – his long back comically upright on the small machine – but the road experience it gave him made transition to a more macho motorbike easy later on. For a darkroom he was allowed to use a small damp lavatory at the Beaford Centre until we could build one of his own at Addisford.

The Beaford Centre was then based in a Victorian rectory, Greenwarren House, in the small roadside village of Beaford. It had two reception rooms and a number of bedrooms which had been converted either into small dormitories for residential courses, or offices for the administrators. In the early days it had a small knot garden, John Lane's creation, and beyond it, an orchard and two old stone barns. Its main deficiency was the lack of either auditorium or gallery. The Music Room, which housed a fine grand piano, could seat only about seventy people, and provided only a small amount of wall space for exhibitions. However, in John's day, when his missionary zeal for bringing life-changing arts to a deprived rural area was in force, performers of international standing, such as the great sitar player, Ravi Shankar, played in that room, and the Alberni String Quartet came regularly to hold a two-week chamber music summer school. Such artists also went out into the community to perform in local venues, schools and churches, for it was a major part of John's vision to take the arts out to the people.

In the 1970s, another ambassador for the Beaford ethos was the peripatetic company of actors, Orchard Theatre, which toured the area and beyond with its own lighting and seating systems – taking classic and home-grown plays, and actors such as Richard Griffiths and Alex Jennings, at the start of their careers, to village halls and schools all over the West Country.

In those days, the Beaford Centre's activities were financed partly by the Dartington Hall Trust, its founder, and partly through regular applications to

South West Arts (the western branch of the Arts Council), Devon County Council, and the two local councils of North Devon, all of which had their own priorities and problems. Funding could not be relied on for more than a year or two at a time, and was therefore a constant worry. It was in the nature of such organisations that staff at the centre were poorly paid, and therefore usually young. They were expected to work long hours, manning evening events all over the district on top of their day jobs in the office. Apart from the director, they had little or no contact with the board of governors who dictated policy.

It was also inevitable that staffing levels, finances and aims would alter continually as time passed, and as public attitudes towards the arts, and the politics of the funding bodies, changed. The Beaford Centre survived some critical moments during James's time there. Now fifty years old, the organisation (renamed Beaford Arts, but no longer based in Beaford) claims to be the longest-running rural arts centre in the country.

8 . STARTING WORK

ARMED WITH A LEICA, the same sort of camera as Cartier-Bresson used, James took his first photographs for the archive in the autumn of 1972. The brief gave him wonderful freedom. Within the loose framework of recording North Devon before it changed, he decided what to take, and did it without any preconceived plan, and without rules or interference from his employer. John Lane, an artist himself, rode the projects he approved of with a light rein. In many ways James was able to work as if he were self-employed.

Finding subjects was not a problem. They were on our very doorstep: the farming going on in the fields that surrounded our cottage; people involved in our day-to-day life; scenes in the streets of our village, Dolton, or in the local towns Torrington and Bideford, where we did our shopping. In addition, we read the local paper to find events to be covered; or heard on the grapevine of intriguing activities about to happen: farm cider making, or rick thatching, or a special seasonal market somewhere. But even if he had no particular subject lined up, James was not concerned. He simply set out and followed his nose, hoping that something worth taking would present itself. It usually did. Sometimes the coincidence of his arrival at a perfect scene was so extraordinary that, agnostic as he was, he would feel he had been 'given' it.

As the project developed in the following spring, we were in the thick of modernising Addisford, using the compensation payment for the London flat. We needed a kitchen and a bathroom. At first James had wanted to add a modernist block which would offset the old building rather than imitate it. I was secretly relieved when the planning people turned that down. Tim Nicholson then produced a traditional, single-storey design with a thatched roof, stable door and deep window embrasures rounded off so as to look as much like the old cob cottage as possible. This got permission. Also, we cut through the sitting room wall to create a lean-to darkroom out of sight at the back. James designed and made the interior of this, going to elaborate lengths to create a worktop out of marine plywood that could resist the constant wetting it would have to endure. He recorded the builders at work for the archive.

He was also busy all over North Devon that first year taking local village scenes, the holiday trade thirty miles away on the north coast beaches of Ilfracombe and Woolacombe, Torrington's May Fair, Holsworthy's horse show, Bideford's Regatta, a Bible Society parade in Hatherleigh, Dolton's and Hatherleigh's autumn carnivals, as well as harvesting and other farm work, markets, trades and shops – including shop facades reminiscent of his father's book *High Street* – and then Christmas displays and customers. With his one hundred and fifth roll of film he rounded off the year by recording the bell-ringers saluting the New Year in Dolton church tower at midnight.

His knowledge of the area rapidly outstripped mine. Over time, he would reduce his longest journeys and concentrate on a patch roughly within a ten-mile radius of Dolton and Beaford; an area that included three towns, Torrington, Hatherleigh and Chulmleigh, and perhaps a dozen villages, as well as miles and miles of small winding lanes. (Devon has more roads than any other county in Britain.) In the end, a good quarter of the archive was taken within the parish of Dolton.

Some months after James started work, we heard the disappointing news that John Lane was resigning as director of the Beaford Centre in order to work thirty miles away at Dartington Hall itself, though he would become one of the centre's governors, and still live locally. It was a blow. Though one of them became a friend, James would not have the same *artistic* rapport with any of John's successors – of whom there were six, and several stand-ins, during his lifetime. It also meant that the informal arrangement he had been working under was formalised by a written contract, albeit a very basic one at first, current for just one year. By the terms of this first document he would receive an annual fee in instalments totalling £500 (worth approximately £5,200 at the time of writing) plus a maximum of £300 for mileage and materials. His negatives would be the property of the Beaford Centre but he could use them privately for his own purposes, with appropriate permission and credit to the archive. The copyright in them would remain his for his lifetime, but negatives and copyright would belong to the Beaford Centre after his death. Such agreements were not unusual before copyright laws changed in 1989. This document was reviewed and expanded, and the salary updated, at intervals throughout his employment at Beaford, as funding for the archive was never secure for long. It was not the easiest of arrangements.

James lived on nervous energy. A recorder of real life needs to be very observant, and very quick to react. He was constantly on the alert for subjects, tense and wide-eyed, and he never went anywhere without one or perhaps two loaded cameras, or extra film and a lightproof bag to change it in. For him there was the excitement of the hunt, that frisson of expectation as he set out of a morning not knowing what he might catch. His main quarry was the traditional under threat, the human story, the beautiful, and anything comic or surreal. He used to describe his work as a kind of tapestry of local life. 'You

see something happening and you say to yourself: I'll have that, and you stitch it in.' As time passed, he developed his skill for spotting – in the heat of the moment – a satisfying geometry in what he saw: the special arrangement of lines and shapes and angles which makes a composition sing.

When we travelled together, as we often did especially in the early days, I shared his excitement. We loved so many of the same things. As passenger, I could keep my eyes peeled for subjects, peering through gateways as we passed, and calling a halt if I spotted something interesting. Invariably, we had our 'bible' with us: Professor W. G. Hoskins's wonderful guide to Devon.

Our secretive countryside lent itself perfectly to this serendipity. Viewed from a hill, it is like a dishevelled green eiderdown quilted with a random network of hedges, and patched here and there with large soft woods and small

View from Harepath, near Beaford, 1980
James Ravilious/Beaford Archive

rags of unkempt thicket. Down in the folds of it one travels more or less blind. The great Devon banks topped with overgrown hedge form a linear copse that blocks the view altogether except at gateways, where one can glimpse blue hills, and the church towers of distant hilltop settlements. The nearer terrain is often completely hidden.

The deep lanes wind like eels, and there is no way of knowing whether the next bend will reveal a modern housing estate, or a hamlet unchanged since before the war. In James's time, an inviting farm track might lead to breeze-block and metal barns, concrete surfaces and the hum of machinery, or to a cobbled yard surrounded by cob-and-thatch buildings from the seventeenth century, where the old way of life went on without power, telephone or even water main. In those days, many of the lanes were so quiet that cows could be

Ashwell Farm with barking dog, Dolton, 1977
James Ravilious/Beaford Archive

left to make their own way back to be milked – shambling slowly home unattended from a distant field, and politely moving up on to the verge if a vehicle did appear.

At home we faced a hanging oak wood on the other side of our small valley; so for distances and skies, James had to climb one of the four steep lanes out of the combe. Once up, he would often turn south-west towards Dartmoor, from where we get most of our weather. Dartmoor features again and again in his pictures. Its profile pens a languid rippling line of low curves and points, a flourish at the end of the landscape that draws the eye irresistibly. Though it only occupies a shallow slice of the view, the moor is a dynamic and variable presence: sometimes the faintest water colour; sometimes bluer than the sky, with a knife edge and a gleaming fringe of cloud; sometimes a glowing

George Ayre feeding sheep in the rain,
Ashwell Farm, Dolton, 1976
James Ravilious/Beaford Archive

promised land. When rain threatens, it doubles in size to become an ominous slate-grey neighbour; while mist, or a travelling shower, erase it altogether.

The high rainfall gives a particular quality to the light of our region, quite unlike the sharp maritime brightness of west Cornwall, for instance. It is more Irish in a way: a soft, misty light that lends an elegiac quality to the landscape, subtle and sad – a challenge to capture on film. And all that rain makes life difficult for cameramen. Soft veils of mist may be evocative; storm clouds can make a splendid backdrop for any foreground interest; and floods transform familiar views into exciting drama; but there are also days and days when the rain just falls relentless out of a dead grey sky. If he was feeling hearty James would go out in this to find some resolute soul who had wrapped himself in a bit of old sacking and stumped off through the sea of mud to tend his stock as usual because he had no choice. Otherwise, James stayed at home in the darkroom and waited till the returning sun lit the braided rivulets glittering down each lane and made the mud glisten like chocolate mousse.

Early morning was his favourite time of day for photography; a good many of his best photos were taken then. The light was low and clear across the landscape, and the emptiness of lane and street gave a significance to any activity he happened on, whether it was a postman on his round or cows coming in to be milked. On a typical day the first light through our low bedroom window would wake him, as it had generations of labourers. I would make him a thermos and some sandwiches while he swallowed a bowl of cornflakes and assembled his kit. Then he set off. In all but the warmest weather, he would be lagged in vest, long johns, workman's shirt, jersey and padded waistcoat, finished with boots, heavy jacket, a scarf, and one of his assortment of dire woolly hats, so it was not easy to manipulate the equipment on top. In the early days when he travelled by scooter or motor-bike, there would be a helmet and leathers too.

Frequently there was a camera bag on each hip slung diagonally across

his chest. Always there was the light meter on a cord around his neck. (Later, spectacles on a cord added to the confusion.) Sod's law often dictated that the right strap was not on top when he needed it in a hurry, which provoked much struggling and cursing, while his subject moved out of view. Not for James the swift anonymous style of Cartier-Bresson, who usually slipped a naked Leica out of his jacket pocket, clicked, and melted away into the crowd.

But then James's working style was a more engaged one from the start. He was part of the community, not an outsider. He didn't want to take people unawares. But he did want them to be living their lives unselfconsciously. So he talked to them; explained about the archive and its purpose, asked if they would mind if he took a few photos for it, and took an interest in whatever they were doing. Then he let them get on with it. It's true that they were

Early morning mist on the River Torridge,
Halsdon, Dolton, 1980
James Ravilious/Beaford Archive

usually unaware of the precise moment when the shutter blinked, but that was because the Leica is such a discreet and quiet camera, and because his fast reactions made it seem that he was doing little more than fiddle with it while he talked. People were more used to having to hold the gaze of an aggressive lens and keep still till the loud crunch, or the flash.

Often he had barely crossed the ford when he encountered our neighbour Archie Parkhouse, a small-holder in his seventies who owned the fields opposite us and rented part of Millhams, the little group of cob-and-stone cottages further along our valley. Most days Archie would be pottering about doing something in an old-fashioned, ramshackle, visually delightful way. To begin with, James felt diffident with him: we hadn't got to know him well yet, and he looked quite daunting. But one wintry day in April 1975 when the two of them had been sheltering from the sleet while Archie checked his flock, James came home and announced: 'I *think* I've got a good one of Archie. We were talking, and I cheekily took it right in his face. I wasn't sure if I dared, but he didn't seem to mind.' Someone had commented that James's subjects were usually in the middle distance, quite often with their backs turned. This portrait, a single spontaneous shot, was a triumphant answer to that accusation of detachment. It was among his very best photographs, and one of his own two favourites.

Archie Parkhouse with ivy for sheep,
Millhams, Dolton, 1975
James Ravilious/Beaford Archive

9 . ARCHIE PARKHOUSE –
PORTRAIT OF A COUNTRYMAN

PEOPLE SAW ARCHIE in remarkably different lights. I had first heard of him from my grandfather who had recruited him into the Dolton Home Guard in 1940. While some had turned up with antique muzzle-loading blunderbusses with which to defend the realm, Archie owned a serviceable shotgun, and was therefore automatically made leader of a six-man patrol (which included my father till he got his call-up papers). To Grandfather, Archie was bit of a rogue, under suspicion of making free with game from the estate. He had not been approved of as a wild-haired (and perhaps not very deferential) young man in the 1920s, when he came courting his future wife, Alice Stokes from Buckingham, who was one of my great-grandfather's maids at Halsdon, and not supposed to have 'followers'.

To some of the local farming people he was a 'character': very good company in the pub, but sometimes exasperating as a neighbour. They claimed his errant sheep ate more of their grass than of his own. Everyone in the neighbourhood knew him. He was a sort of celebrity at Hatherleigh livestock market

Archie Parkhouse by lamplight,
Millhams, Dolton, c. 1980
James Ravilious

(which he had attended regularly since the age of ten when he had to go with his grandfather in order to drive him home in the pony cart after long post-market sessions in the pub); and most of the indigenous population for miles around had encountered him in at least one of his former roles: village foot-baller, farm labourer, road mender, wartime rabbit trapper, or licensed slaughterer of pigs.

We, however, were rather in awe of him to begin with, and anxious to keep in his good books. To us he was an impressive figure: a grand old man, a symbol, an embodiment, of the traditional way of life that James was trying to capture; and absolutely typical of the local character: stubborn, but also friendly and playful. Planted in the lane in one of his terrible hats, with a ragged green cardigan, trousers and braces straining over an imposing stomach, he would light up his pipe and launch into a rambling dissertation on times past 'back in they days', which would keep one spellbound for hours. His rabbit-trapping (and perhaps other more covert activities) had taken him out and about in the fields at dawn in several local parishes; he knew every hedge of them by heart. He would tell of strange wildlife encounters: the rabbit he watched climbing a tree to escape a fox; the salmon marooned in a drought-shrunk pool which he caught with his bare hands. (Later, his dogs stole it from him.) Or he would recall working on an outstanding crop that had been grown in a neighbour's field fifty years before. Every yard of the valley reminded him of some event, usually comic, which had happened there in his lifetime. If a car passed (which was fairly rare in those days) he would peer in in the confident expectation of knowing the driver, his history, and everyone he was related to. He could read the weather, and talk about the local animals and birds, using the lovely old Devon names for some of them. I found it delightful to be addressed as 'My dear soul!' or, even better, 'My dear maid!' – 'maid' was still an affectionate term in North Devon for a female of any age or status. His language was almost Shakespearean at times. I remember a description of a man who was so bandy-legged that ''ee couldn' stop a pig in a passage' and, more poetical, someone so emaciated by illness that ''ee's no more'n a rasher of wind'. But Archie's tales were often hard to follow both because of the strong dialect, with its curiously transposed pronouns (''Er wouldn' spake to the likes of we') and because many of the actors in them had playground nicknames which had stuck with them ever since boyhood. Most of Archie's stories were funny: tales of mischievous doings in his youth – outwitting irate farmers, stealing their precious tar barrels for Bonfire Night – all laced with his special laugh that sizzled like bacon frying in a pan. Defying authority was clearly a favourite sport.

A classic adventure was his encounter up at Halsdon House with my disabled and eccentric great-grandfather at dusk one evening in the 1920s. Archie had had his forbidden tryst with Alice at the back of the house, and was taking a risky short cut home through the ornamental shrubbery at the front, when he was caught out by Great-Grandfather emerging, as he often did at that time of day, with a dog and a shotgun to keep down the rabbits. Archie dived into a clump of azaleas and waited on all fours. Unfortunately the dog discovered him and, in spite of Archie's whispered curses, 'pointed' eagerly. Calling him off, Great-Grandfather fired a spray of shot into the bushes, which grazed Archie's backside. There was nothing he could do but suffer in silence until Great-Grandfather went indoors.

Archie had a presence that made him superbly photogenic; and he accepted the camera without self-consciousness. He loved company, and soon came to approve of 'Ol' Jimmy' recording his life, making no bones about intimate things like his shaving, or his unmade bed with chamber pot beneath, being photographed for posterity, because he saw the point of it.

We grew to love him, and to have a neighbourly relationship that was typical of the old country ways. He used to put his lambing ewes in the scruffy little fields over the stream opposite our garden and, though no farmer, I learnt to spot ewes in difficulties, or deserted lambs, and would go round to tell Archie of the problem. He and Ivor Brock, his neighbour and assistant, would turn out, grumbling, and deliver a wedged lamb, or take a rejected one into a shed with its mother to persuade them to bond. A day or two later, there would be an anonymous gift in the milk crate at the end of our lane: some enormous earthy leeks wrapped in the *Farmers' Weekly*, or potatoes or eggs in a second-hand paper bag, to repay the debt. (Not that *I* saw it as a debt, of course. My reasons for helping were sentimental ones about the welfare of the animals.) The touching thing was that the not-very-bright-looking ewes with their myopic shaggy faces learnt to look to me for help. When they were in trouble they would come down to the bank of the stream and gaze across at our cottage appealing for aid. One even summoned me insistently in the middle of a cold moonlit night in March because her lamb had fallen in and been swept away to a ledge under a high bank twenty yards downstream.

There were other occasions for Archie's company. We took him once to Bampton Pony Fair on Exmoor, a big annual gathering for the locality. He came dressed in his three-piece smart occasions suit and homburg hat, and enjoyed himself like a boy on an outing from school, commenting on every-thing we passed during the journey, and holding court with old acquaintance when we arrived. A trip of thirty miles was an adventure for people like him who hardly ever went further than the annual County Show in Exeter in all their lives.

Also, he and James shared the same birthday: 22 August, though there were thirty-six years between them. (By a neat coincidence, James's hero Henri Cartier-Bresson was also born on that date.) James would go round to Mill-hams to celebrate, reluctantly accepting a tumbler-full of whisky which he didn't like or have the head for. Archie in his cups was a rather magnificent sight: very merry, and rosy of face, and somehow rather biblically larger than life.

After a while, Alice became very ill with a cancer that I suspect she had neglected too long because of the old country dread of hospitals (which were still tainted by the reputation of the workhouse). Eventually, she was treated in the brand new North Devon Hospital in Barnstaple. Archie would come round to us to find out how she was doing. He had no telephone himself, and was reluctant to use one, so I made calls on his behalf. He also asked me once to go with him to visit her as he was clearly ill at ease in such places.

When she died, he came over to tell us. I saw him standing waiting for me as usual under the huge elm tree by the stream, and I waded across. He said formally: 'I'm sorry to have to tell you Alice passed away last night.' But then as I tried to comfort him, he said sorrowfully: ''Er suffered. 'Er did suffer, poor ol' maid!'

Some time later, he teamed up with two drinking companions from Dolton, friends he had known since childhood, and took to travelling for the first time in his life. Together the trio of widowers, all in their seventies, made coach trips to Scotland, Jersey and even to Malta, where it is clear from holiday snaps that they had a wonderful time, observing different sorts of farming, trying new drinks, and being fêted by the locals. We would receive a postcard addressed to 'Mr & Mrs James and Robin' – Archie couldn't cope with Ravilious – with a brief message in his curiously disconnected script: 'We are having a very nice time & the sun is shining lovely. Cheers, Archie.' His first ever passport photo, which he commissioned from James for the Malta trip, went into the archive.

Millhams cottages had no amenities. In his last years Archie was reluctantly persuaded to move up West Lane to the edge of the village to live in a more convenient home, Horseshoe Cottage, which he actually owned. He found the valley hard to leave. He resisted the move for months on the grounds that he didn't want to live where everyone would know his business. Having moved, however, he spent quite a large part of his time leaning on his garden wall to watch the world go by, and engaging it in conversation as it passed. But his heart was still in the valley, which was hardly surprising. He had lived in one or other part of it all his life – born in one cottage, walking the lane twice a day from before the age of five as he went to and from school, moving to live with his grandfather on an old farm at the far end when he was about ten, honeymooning with Alice for a year in our cottage, Addisford, and then renting the Millhams one for the rest of their life together in order to be close to the fields his grandfather had left him. In over seventy years he would have absorbed the very essence of this one tiny piece of country: its seasons, its changing lights, its wildlife, its smells; noting each year, with the top of his mind, the growing of the grass, the ewes swelling with lamb, the thistles in need of a scythe; but also, more subliminally perhaps, the wild cherry trees lighting up each spring at the wood's edge across the stream; and the yellow-hammer singing its drowsy little ditty from that hedgerow thorn in West Lane, summer after summer. As they still do.

Archie lived for several years in the village house, helped by Jo Curzon, his former Millhams neighbour. She used to drive him down every morning to see the stock he still kept in his fields. Eventually, he too got cancer, and spent his last months in the cottage hospital in Torrington where my mother died.

James took more pictures of Archie than anyone else, apart from family; enough for us to make an entire exhibition devoted to him later on. If a tough old countryman can be such a thing, Archie was James's muse. His death hit him hard. He said he felt a light had gone out of our valley.

Archie taking leave of his valley, Millhams, Dolton, c. 1984
James Ravilious

10 . OLD FARMING WAYS

FOR PEOPLE OF ARCHIE'S SORT it was a hard life. They had grown up
through lean times during the First World War. In 1917, two years after Archie
would have left school aged twelve, an official report by the Board of Agricul-
ture found that the farm labourer was the 'hardest-worked, lowest-paid, worst-
fed and clothed, and worst-housed class of the whole British community.' They
had learned from an early age to be prepared for unforeseen trouble, and did
not spend cash willingly. By the 1970s they were old men, set in their ways,
and their output was often too small to justify modern labour-saving equipment. Many were tenants, not owners, so that though they might care deeply
for the land they worked, its long-term future was out of their hands. (For that
matter, few of their landlords had much free cash to spend either, in those
days.) Living mostly in 'tied' homes, if they couldn't afford a rise in the rent
they had to move on. Sometimes a tenant smallholder would inherit a few
fields or, if the legacy was in capital, would invest it in a rundown cottage going
cheap. Archie did both. But he would only very reluctantly spend it on new
machinery, or longterm maintenance. Vets' bills were cut to the minimum by

using old home remedies; and sheds and equipment subsided slowly into dis-repair, even if that caused more trouble in the end. If hungry stock escaped through a badly maintained hedge, the gap was darned with binder twine, or plugged with a Victorian brass bedstead decommissioned in the 1940s when mass-produced wooden furniture came in. But the mend was only a temporary measure. Better hedge maintenance in the first place, or adequate feed for the animals, might have been more cost-effective. Archie and Ivor spent days wandering the lanes looking for escaped sheep.

The old methods made for interesting photography. They were also kinder to the countryside in some ways. For instance, few of the smallholders could afford to drench their soil in chemicals, even if they had wanted to, so a diversity of flowers flourished. Archie's Addisford fields were full of lady's

Archie and friends dragging home a sick ram,
Millhams, Dolton, 1976
James Ravilious/Beaford Archive

smock in April. And in the summer when he didn't get round to cutting the thistles, they flowered in five-foot-high forests, hedge to hedge, alive with goldfinches and butterflies – Marbled Whites and Clouded Yellows, as well as all the common ones. (Though that couldn't be called good husbandry, and was unpopular with some of his neighbours.)

Short of money and labour, people just trudged on, 'getting by'. But it would be wrong to call them depressed. It was their way of life, not just a job, and they were deeply connected to the place, and their animals. They took the hardships in their stride, living by the stoic philosophy: 'We have to take what comes, and work around it.' It was the only way they had to cope with the vagaries of the weather, and all the other problems of infectious disease, market fluctuations and government directives, over which they were powerless. And

Archie and his dog Sally in a lane
near Millhams, Dolton, 1982
James Ravilious/Beaford Archive

they would speak with contempt of 'they silly buggers' up in London who tried to tell them what to do. Again, in *Moortown Diary*, Ted Hughes describes the character of the natives of this small pocket of England – a character which he found unique. 'The isolated self-sufficiency of the old North Devon farmers was something else altogether, like nothing I had ever encountered.'[3]

Modern agriculturalists don't admire this style of farming – and certainly it contravened all sorts of regulations now in place about health and safety, and animal welfare. James was aware that the country people he photographed had a complex attitude towards animals: a genuine affection for certain creatures, especially those that had been hand-reared, for instance; but also a ruthless matter-of-factness about others. Archie was fond of his old cow, and of his dogs: Sally, the elegant collie, three-legged after an accident, but still

Hounds killing a fox near Hatherleigh, 1975
James Ravilious/Beaford Archive

nimble enough to round up the flock, and Bob, the black mongrel, whose only talent was barking. And he would sit in his shed for hours stroking a crippled hen on his lap while he talked. But his sheep sometimes had to hobble about on their knees because of foot rot or rheumatism; and James recorded him and Ivor grimly triumphant over the bedraggled corpse of the fox which had been killing their poultry. It had suffered a slower death than the hens, writhing in Archie's hedgerow snare all night, a wide scar in the bank stark evidence of its long struggle. On the other hand, Archie, having been a licensed pig-slaughterer for a time, was angrier than I had ever seen him when someone botched the illegal home slaughter of an animal.

James's stomach for the cruder side of farming life was not robust. Some things made him squeamish. He drew the line at recording the toughest procedures. He would take the arrival of a lamb or a calf (though he was clearly reluctant to attend the birth of our first child, Ben, and secretly relieved to be excused from my next two deliveries). He felt obliged to record the fate of another fox being pulled apart by a posse of hounds, because hunting was such a historic and controversial issue. But he turned away from extremes like the dismembering of a lamb stuck inside its mother, in order to extract it piecemeal and save her life. Such things went on but he couldn't make pictures of them.

11 . JAMES'S PEOPLE

JAMES NEVER DROVE ANYWHERE in our local patch without people in gateways, and village streets, and other vehicles, saluting him cheerfully as we passed. Some were neighbours we saw regularly; others were friends he had made at random in the course of his work.

One of the nearest was Ivor Brock who lived in another of the Millhams cottages, just beyond Archie's. He spent a lot of his time with Archie, either helping, or just chatting. The two of them were usually to be found out and about together – Ivor with a Woodbine stub, and Archie redolent of Golden Virginia tobacco, both equally dishevelled in appearance. Ivor was quiet and retiring, a spear-bearer to Archie's leading role. When he did speak, it was with the distinctive high, fruity tone and diphthong vowels of the Devon voice. (He pronounced 'gate' 'gay-et'.) One couldn't get to know him as easily as Archie, but at Christmastime if he met one of our children in the road he would shyly put a shilling in their palm.

Olive Bennett was also a 'character', in some ways a female counterpart to Archie, with the same toughness, the same defiant spirit. She had not had

an easy life, I think, doing heavy farmwork from an early age for her grand-parents, her mother and her autocratic father, and then finally on her own, in primitive conditions which led, as so often, to crippling rheumatism. She was fiercely independent, defying all officialdom, and stubbornly stonewalling the neighbouring landowner's legal attempts to increase the rate on the fields she rented from him. She talked in a fast choppy style and the broadest of Devon accents – swearing freely, but in a cheerful sort of way. James loved to record her tumbledown arrangements at Cupper's Piece, and the fine horned cattle she kept on Beaford Moor, the bit of unimproved moorland common next to her cottage. Her beasts always seemed to arrange themselves in delightfully eighteenth-century poses. Olive welcomed a chat with James, though she claimed she used to try to dodge his camera. I think she was secretly pleased

Ivor Brock, Millhams, Dolton, 1975
James Ravilious/Beaford Archive

to know her portrait had become famous. Some years after he died she said to me, 'Poor ol' James! I thought the world of 'im.'

George Ayre was my grandfather's tenant at Ashwell Farm. For many years he lived there in bachelor disarray, a gentle smiling man with gap teeth, and an almost impenetrable Devon accent. The farm had a rather sad and derelict look when James first photographed it. But in mid-life George married Winifred, an art teacher from Leicester, who loved the beautiful old place and its romantic setting even more than we did. The view down on to it, and beyond to the Torridge valley, was one of James's favourites, especially when evening light gilded the distant hills across the valley, and picked out the pinnacles of Merton church tower. When he went to and from work or meetings at the Beaford Centre, he passed the top of Ashwell lane, and would stop yet

Olive Bennett and her Red Devon cattle,
Cupper's Piece, Beaford, 1979
James Ravilious/Beaford Archive

again to take George at work in his fields with that wonderful backdrop, or the sturdy old earth building itself beneath its thick rug of thatch, embraced by woods and the gleaming curl of river beyond.

Another neighbour was Alf Pugsley who farmed Lower Langham Farm on the high ground at the far end of our valley. He was a traditionalist, keen to transmit the old skills. He taught Stephen Squire, the young man he employed, to 'steep', or lay his hedges in the way they had been done probably ever since our Anglo-Saxon forebears first carved their settlements out of the forest. Alf could tell you the different qualities of hedgerow trees, how they cut, how they bent, how they re-grew to make an impermeable barrier. And he would keep his hedges vigorous by 'casting up', shovelling up the sludge from the ditch on to the bank to refresh the hedge's growth, and by 'clatting',

George Ayre with thatching reed
at Ashwell Farm near Dolton, 1973
James Ravilious/Beaford Archive

plastering squares of turf from the edge of the field on to the sides of the bank to hold it in place. This sort of care had been commonplace before the Great War when there was plenty of cheap labour in need of a winter job, but it was far too labour-intensive for most farmers to keep going in our time. By then, most hedges were regularly savaged by a hired mechanical cutter, or else left to flourish untamed until they were no longer barriers at all – hence the dishevelment of our particular countryside. Alf preserved the traditions because he felt strongly about these things, and he was glad that James was there to record them.

A more unworldly Devon character was Henry Bright who lived in Beaford. He and his wife Pat ran a taxi service which was invaluable to us, both before we had a car, and afterwards if James was unavailable to drive me to a

Alf Pugsley 'casting up',
Langham, Dolton, 1978
James Ravilious/Beaford Archive

train or appointment. Henry also broke in young horses as a hobby, with a gentleness which worked wonders on even the most difficult. Driving with Henry was always an adventure. He was a born naturalist, all his knowledge learned from close observation of the wildlife he loved. As he drove he would be pouring out a stream of detailed observations on what we passed: how rooks build their nests, for example, or the behaviour of moles. I remember a typical Henry trip when he came to fetch me from our distant railway station one snowy winter night, and on the high ground near High Bickington we found a hare running desperately up the road ahead of us because it couldn't get through a wire fence. Henry, alight with excitement, stopped the car. Then, as if in a scene from a Hardy novel, we crunched about on the snow in the headlamps' beam till the hare was gently shepherded under a gate.

Henry Bright training a young horse, Beaford, 1978
James Ravilious/Beaford Archive

Though many of his subjects were elderly, James didn't ignore the young. Children at school or play, or in fancy dress, often feature in the archive. And he had a soft spot for pretty girls. It was typical of him to find a Leonardo angel, Marilyn Bourne, filling crates for the family milk round in Beaford. Some locals were rich sources of information. Bill Cooke was one such authority. A thoughtful, elderly Devon bachelor who farmed alone at Colehouse near Riddlecombe, breeding the cattle and donkeys he loved as if they were his children, he had spent his spare time absorbing a library of old books about North Devon's past. Margaret Bolt, who still farms with her family at Week, near Burrington, is another. She completely understood the importance of the archive as social history. As she recorded in her own reminiscences, *When We Came to Week,* she comes from a long line of local farmers. She could talk to James in detail about the local agricultural history her ancestors had lived through. She would think to call him when they were lambing at Week, or when an old cider press was going into action, or when the bulldozer was coming for an old cob cottage by the road. People like her are themselves living archives of farming life in this part of the world, their knowledge and skills a heritage which should be valued.

Other helpful contacts were the two local doctors James shadowed for a while in the early 1980s: Paul Bangay, a partner at the Torrington Health Centre where we were patients, and Richard Westcott of South Molton. Both asked James to record their work for articles they were writing on life as a rural GP, and James welcomed the opportunities. He followed Paul and Richard on their rounds – those were the days when doctors made regular house calls. With the patients' consent, he was able to hover in the background taking fascinating interiors and intimate scenes, without either doctor or patient remembering he was there. In his mind was the documentary work he admired by the American photographers Walker Evans, who recorded sharecropper lives in Alabama during the Great Depression, and Eugene Smith, who made a

Marylyn Bourne loading milk bottles, Beaford, 1983
James Ravilious/Beaford Archive

Bill Cooke with his cat,
Colehouse, Riddlecombe, 1988
James Ravilious/Beaford Archive

moving photo-essay on the work of a black midwife in rural Carolina in the 1950s. Not that James saw the same degree of poverty as the Americans, but the situations he encountered were often just as touchingly intimate, and the pictures he was able to take pay tribute to the close relationships which often existed then between doctor and patient.

As a craftsman himself, he was always drawn to others: hedgers, basket makers, a printer, a saddler, a monumental mason, the carpenters who worked on our house, people like thatcher Bill Hammond, a shy reclusive man whom James would encounter on roofs and wheat ricks all over the area, or visit when he made cider in the little shed at the back of his lovely old longhouse, Rashleigh Mill, near Chulmleigh. James enjoyed drawing out skilled people on their crafts, their tools and their histories.

Dr Paul Bangay visiting an elderly patient in bed,
Langtree, 1981
James Ravilious/Beaford Archive

When he was on the road, the time would come for refreshments. Sometimes I'd made a picnic, but James preferred junk food and its environment. In a café he would always choose a seat with a view both into the room and out of the window, if possible. While he downed his cheeseburger, fries and Coca-Cola, his large eyes would be quietly resting on fellow diners and passers-by, as he thought about their lives and characters, and made pictures of them in his head.

He was forever exploring. It was constantly surprising how much there always was left to discover in such a small territory, even after years of work. Returning from a trip, perhaps to the shops or the dentist in Torrington, one of us would ask, 'Have we ever been down there?' and James would swing over and plunge into yet another green tunnel little wider than the car. Sometimes it was fruitless; but often we found new subjects this way, and ended up guzzling tea and lavish cakes with strangers who were happy to reminisce for hours, and to have James record an old building, craft or custom which they had kept going. It was a two-way relationship. He got his pictures (not to mention the cake); they got the comfort of knowing that their way of life would not disappear without trace.

One of his best pictures came about by such random exploration. He had been asked to record an event on Exmoor one evening in May 1985 – a folk group in a pub – and had decided to make a day of it as it was beyond his normal terrain. Nosing about for subjects in unfamiliar country, he came upon Dick French and his family shearing, and as usual got into conversation while photographing them. It was Cup Final day, and even farmers took time off to watch that historic event on TV. James was invited in for a cuppa, and as so often took the opportunity to observe the observers, as well as watching the game himself. The artist Robert Organ wrote of this picture:

> The French family watching the Cup Final – what a wonderful image this is, impossible to look at without smiling. Within the old farmhouse walls they sit

absorbed by a spectacle which is withheld from us, each in a zone of personal space, each uniquely individual – the psychology and body language is compelling. Yet they are bound together in their preoccupation and the wonderful compositional sense tells us of this – for there is a web of connections throughout the picture; every shape, line, and edge seems locked in its correct position so that nothing can be added or subtracted from this unity.

How this is achieved from the ceaseless flux of living reality is for me an intangible mystery – and what intuition informed him to press the exposure button at the very micro second when Mr French lowered his tea mug and Mrs French raised her right hand?[4]

Dick French and his family watching the Cup Final,
Brendon Barton, Exmoor, 1985
James Ravilious/Beaford Archive

For someone as unassuming as James, handling his human subjects was not a problem. The comfortable interaction between him and those he photographed is manifest in many of his portraits. Often the subjects are looking thoughtfully back into the past, but even in those pictures where they are looking straight at him, though they may not be smiling, you can usually see that there is an easy dialogue going on, for James could talk to almost anyone. It was second nature to him to strike up a conversation with strangers anywhere – in trains, in queues, at a field gate – without any conventional preamble; and they would respond, even if they couldn't always follow his idiosyncratic train of thought. He had a pleasant tenor voice, and a diffident friendliness which quickly disarmed all but the most curmudgeonly. After an initial chat, he would leave people to get on with their work; and many of them testify that they completely forgot what he was doing, and were amazed later on when they saw the pictures he had taken. With others, he asked questions while he clicked away in his casual fashion. Some of the farmers must have thought him an ignorant townie to begin with, but their working days were solitary and they appreciated having a genuine listener to talk to. In any case, it seems to be characteristic of West Country people to be friendly to strangers, and to relish talking about the old days. Recalling who did what was clearly a major pastime before television arrived, and presumably had been since pre-history.

But James was always anxious not to intrude. For example, he very regretfully decided not to record the funeral of Dolton's ninety-year-old blacksmith and captain of the bell-ringers, Reuben Clements. The entire male population of the village turned out for that in the sombre glory of dark suits and homburg hats, and it could have made a tremendous photograph, but James felt it would be insensitive to bring a camera. He was pleased and flattered if people invited him to cover their more private moments, such as a farmer's daughter getting ready for her wedding, or a family christening party.

He met with almost no opposition when he was at work. House-proud housewives sometimes begged to be allowed to smarten up their homes for the camera, but he persuaded them that it was ordinary life, not Sunday best, that the archive needed most. Well-born ladies could be a challenge because they professed to hate being photographed, or because they were nervous of their valuables being advertised to burglars, but James could charm the feistiest Indian Army wife: they were from the same mould as his Garwood grandmother. He would bring up some detail from Grandpa Garwood's diaries, and the old days in Poonah would unfold while the shutter blinked and blinked. In all his years of work for the archive, James was refused permission to photograph only twice. And though his franker portraits make others laugh, their subjects never seemed to take offence at them because they looked on James as a friend.

I imagine they formed the same first impression as I did at that party in 1969: that he was an amusing eccentric. Why would anyone want to photograph farmyard muck being shovelled? But after he died they would tell me they felt 'very fortunate to have known such a lovely man'. They liked his courtesy, and soon warmed, as I had done, to his genuine interest in them. Later they came to value his work, attending his slide-shows and exhibitions, and buying his books with a certain proprietorial pride. They smartened up after the evening milking and came in crowds to his private view parties to find themselves and their acquaintance in his pictures, and to tease each other about what he had caught them doing.

His images had a more profound effect on them, too. His love of the landscape and his rapport with its people, so clearly seen in his work, gave them what John Lane first envisaged, a sense of their countryside's identity as a special place: not just a rundown backwater where life was a struggle, but a precious piece of old England worthy to be looked at intently, and evaluated, before it disappeared. Somewhere that could even, perhaps, offer lessons for

the future. As John wrote, 'The Beaford Archive, belonging to its future and rooted in its past, is also of and for North Devon in the most fundamental sense.' George Stoneman, who farmed in Riddlecombe, put it another way: 'The thing about James is, he makes our lives seem important.' Many people have told me that they looked at their familiar territory with new eyes after seeing James's view of it.

George Stoneman, Skellies, Riddlecombe, 1975
James Ravilious/Beaford Archive

12 . THE YEAR

SPRING WAS PROBABLY James's favourite season. Its light penetrated the bare woods, and pencilled the sides of wet tree trunks like an engraved line on glass. The low angle cast long shadows across the fields making useful horizontals to compose with. If there had been a frost, the grey bloom of it lingered in those shadows – and even, briefly, after they had moved – while rain, frost or dew made the soft sparkle he worked hard to capture.

He also loved the abundance of flowers in a Devon spring: constellations of snowdrops, primroses clustered along the hedgebanks, and the embroidery of mingled pink, white and blue as campion, stitchwort and bluebells follow. Their effect reminded him of the mediaeval tapestries he so much enjoyed. But unlike me he was no botanist. I used to tease him, a little unfairly, with not knowing a daisy from a dandelion. In return, he mocked my passionate interest by inventing silly names for the flowers I found, such as 'Herod's Knee'.

Towards the end of May, some warm sunny morning, we would become aware of a hubbub in the far corner of Archie's field across the stream: shouts, barking, and the anxious outcry of sheep combined with the phut-phut-phut

Archie Parkhouse and friends shearing,
Addisford, Dolton, 1981
James Ravilious/Beaford Archive

of his greasy old Lister engine. It was shearing time again. The little machine lived by the hedge all year under a bit of tarpaulin, and needed much coaxing and swearing to bring it back to life. It was, I think, the only machine that Archie owned after he gave up his motorbike many years before. Anything else was borrowed for a specific task, or else the work was done by hand.

The scene was irresistible, bringing back the old days when farming was a sociable affair. There were always four or five people involved, and others passing by got drawn in too. Archie, in shirt sleeves and braces, supervised and handed out the beer, while his neighbour Jo Curzon and various young men did most of the hard graft, wrestling the struggling animals to the ground, and bending over at a back-breaking angle to peel off the fleeces on to a big sheet of polythene spread out by the gate. The air was thick with a reek like burning kippers from the dung and hot oil. When Archie's own small flock had been undressed and removed, Alf Pugsley's sheep would join the party. They came down the lane from his farm at Langham, as part of the reciprocal arrangement between the two neighbours: Archie's flock went up to Langham to be dipped in Alf's tank; Alf's came down to Millhams to be sheared.

By July the landscape could be more challenging photographically. Its lines became blurred by the almost tropical growth, and the best of the flowers were over. Also the light had changed. The sun overhead made shorter shadows, and was often muted by a sullen humid haze that flattened everything. The oak woods which had glowed so rich and crisp in spring now took on a uniform texture like clustered broccoli. James used to find our combe a little claustrophobic. He would begin to grumble about 'all that *green*', and yearn for France, or the smooth bare flanks of the Sussex Downs.

Luckily, the summer provided plenty of other subjects. Now he would be alert for news of fêtes and fairs, sports days and gymkhanas, where he could be seen dodging about in a comic white cotton hat, braces and the open sandals *with socks* which would mortify his son in later years, as he recorded

the events and, more particularly, the observers of the events. He must have puzzled other cameramen sometimes by the way he turned his back on the platform, or the finishing tape, in order to record the onlookers instead. It was a chance to get a whole community at its most relaxed. And he particularly liked to capture the preparations for events: cardiganed ladies assessing sheaves of flowers for their church vases, or handmaidens preparing a carnival queen for her starring role.

Summer also offered scenes of the various harvests that crown the farming year: damasked swathes of grass mown for hay; or the comic architecture of straw bales; and, in particular, our special local crop, wheat 'reed' for thatching. This was a gift for James as the wheat is cut and treated by traditional methods to preserve the length of the straws, and so creates a landscape

Wilf Pengelly setting up stooks,
Woolleigh Barton, Beaford, 1974
James Ravilious/Beaford Archive

that harks back to the distant past: row upon row of tousled stooks, their sheaves lolling together under the weight of ripe grain, defining contours as they dwindle towards a distant hedge. Apart from their bindings, corn stooks seem hardly to have changed in their design over the centuries. James had pictures by mediaeval illuminators, Breughel, Gainsborough and Samuel Palmer in mind as he recorded them.

These stooks can still be seen in North Devon, but no longer, as James saw them, being stored in traditional ricks, some of which were even thatched in the old way in his day. Months later this would be followed by another picturesque event, the dismantling of those ricks for threshing. The rickety wooden vehicle, the 'reed-comber', almost as big as a London bus and painted in faded pink and scarlet, would totter along the road and set up beside the

Reedcombing at Westacott, Riddlecombe, 1974
James Ravilious/Beaford Archive

ricks. In its heyday it had been powered by a steam engine; in James's time it was driven by a belt from a stationary tractor. Its task was to thresh off the grain and rubbish, then straighten and tie the straws into 'nitches', the bundles which thatchers use. There was a lot of noise and dust and cheerful banter, for the operation needed many hands; and then, as the lowest level of the rick was reached, there would be a ferocious rat-hunt by terriers.

The final crop of the year was apples. In the overgrown orchards people would be out bagging windfalls and carting them off to Inch's, the local cider producer in Winkleigh, or possibly to one of the ancient cider presses made of oak which still presided in dark sheds on some old farms – relics of the days when labourers in the area went to work on home-grown cider, part of their wages being paid in it.

Filling sacks with apples, West Park, Iddesleigh, 1986
James Ravilious/Beaford Archive

In the autumn the light usually became crisper, and now there might be a woolly serpent of mist over the river in the early morning, which James would take from a hilltop, or plunge down into for a ghostly landscape emerging through the melting vapour. Soon the hanging woods would begin to glow again, but this time with the smouldering tints of spice: turmeric, cinnamon and paprika. Then there might be the low, golden light of winter to work with, when the landscape was at its simplest and framed, like a gothic window, by the tracery of bare oaks. Eventually, if he was lucky, there might be the exciting graphics of snow.

We seldom got more than a sugaring of snow in our mild climate, but James always made the most of it, rushing off as far as Exmoor or Dartmoor if they were looking white. But the winter of 1977/8 was exceptional. Snow fell before Christmas, and again afterwards, with blizzards to whip it into immense wind-smoothed waves against hedge and building, which then froze there because of the intense cold. All lanes were blocked to traffic. Dolton was completely cut off for ten days and life moved back several decades into the past. We fetched unpasteurised milk in jugs from the farm, and pulled goods on sledges as North Devonians did for centuries before we had adequate roads. People were out and about in a festive mood, and being neighbourly.

It was less glamorous for farmers, however. They had to find and dig out their lambing ewes, and get feed and water to all their animals, in savage conditions. James was determined to record their hardships as well as the pretty scenes. It is worth pointing out that for every well-known picture of a farmer trudging through the drifts and grimacing in the wind, there was also a photographer in front of him with fingers almost too cold to work the camera button.

The cold was so extreme and prolonged that winter that a buzzard fed regularly on the bird table six feet from our sitting room window; and in between feeds, blackbirds, thrushes, chaffinches – even redwings – packed themselves in a row on the windowsill, pressed against the glass for a little share of our Rayburn's warmth.

It was an exciting time for James. I only saw him when darkness fell and he came home hungry and worn out. He had covered miles each day, often walking the countryside laboriously on top of the hedges because if he stepped off on to the gleaming crust of snow it crushed like meringue and engulfed him up to his chest.

Ivor Brock rescuing a lamb in a blizzard,
Millhams, Dolton, 1978
James Ravilious/Beaford Archive

13 . DEVELOPMENTS

THOSE EARLY YEARS were good. The row of black negative files expanded; we explored; we made friends; and we got involved in local happenings; while I learned to grow handsome vegetables in our rich valley soil, and developed a passion for old-fashioned cottage flowers, auriculas especially. The countryside which had always seemed 'home' to me enveloped James too, and I think became the roots which his fractured childhood had denied him.

When we planned our move to Devon we had both been concerned that we might miss the culture of London; but the country had absorbed us at once, and we just forgot about films and shows and galleries. Rural life was so much more intimate; and the sense of discovery we lived with, of the land-scape and its people because of James's work, and of the wildlife around us, erased all hankerings for a metropolitan existence.

Cottage life resonated for us both with our happiest childhood memo-ries. For James, it brought back the early days with his mother in Essex, and later escapes to Furlongs and Barra. For me, my time at Halsdon Mill as a very young child had worked what Charles Morgan in *A Breeze of Morning* calls 'my deep magics'. Moonlight glowing on flaky lime plaster, the piercing vibrato of a wren on the windowsill, the mellow clack of a latch, the scent of early woodsmoke drifting up the stairs, made for me a poetry too deep to put into words – and it was further gilded by the legend of *my* mother living and loving there before my birth.

We responded to the buildings themselves, to the maternal comfort of cob and thatch (warm in winter, cool in summer – dark and womb-like always); and to the sense that they had been shaped from the natural ingredients to hand in the immediate countryside: stones, clay, dung, oak, hazel and wheat straw, rather than alien materials, using techniques handed down from pre-history. Because they heaved and subsided a little as the cob first dried, such buildings had an organic quality, as if they had grown out of the ground. They made one feel closer to the natural world than other types of house. And the natural world seemed to share the feeling. At Addisford, wrens roosted under the eaves in winter; a shrew hoovered the kitchen floor; pipistrelles squabbled in the porch roof in hot weather; and hornets boomed in and out of the thatch – all to a backing track of birdsong, and the quiet conversation of the stream.

But both of us knew by experience that the rural idyll comes at a price: hard physical work. This gave James insight into the world of the country people he photographed. Their daily lives might be picturesque in his viewfinder, but he never romanticised them. He knew first-hand about draughts, damp sheets and calloused hands; what it was to get up in a dark, unheated cottage, to have to pump water, light a stove, and wait twenty minutes for a kettle to boil, and to visit an outside lavatory in an icy wind, just as he knew what it was to work long and hard with a shovel or a saw. His time at Furlongs in Sussex and Higgins House on Barra had taught him that. He didn't know a great deal about farm work, but he understood and respected the dogged commitment of tending animals day in day out and of labouring all day in all weathers, and the craftsman's satisfaction in a manual job done well.

He also knew what it was like to live on a small and unpredictable income. Though my grandfather's gift of the cottage had made us privileged compared with many of the people round us, money was always scarce, and sudden huge bills, for thatching, or car, or camera, would take us unawares. I worried more than James did about this; he thought about money as little as possible, whether he had any or not, and didn't open bank statements. On the rare occasions when we had a windfall – usually a kind family gift or legacy – he could think of three ways to spend it, none of which involved saving for the future. He couldn't see the point of that. If life was so uncertain, why not enjoy it while one could? When we found ourselves in dire straits he would suggest a defiantly expensive treat 'to cheer us up'.

In 1973 we decided to start a family, and I became pregnant, which provided James with a useful entrée into the clinics and anti-natal classes I had to attend. The following February, when I went into labour, he followed me into the Barnstaple hospital on the motorbike. But when things got medical and the midwives suggested he leave, he went off gratefully to photograph the hospital's new IVF clinic, returning just in time to greet his son. We called him simply Ben, feeling that a surname as difficult as Ravilious needed the plainest of first names.

At that point we had to upgrade our transport. The motorbike was no longer adequate. I had ridden pillion until heavily pregnant, but it was useless once Ben was on the scene. So then we moved up another notch. The fibreglass three-wheeler Reliant Robin had recently come on the market, and at that time had the peculiar advantage of being drivable with only a motorcycle licence, despite its four seats. It was also relatively cheap. With that name, and those benefits, we felt it was only right that we should have one – and a scarlet one, at that – even if it did bob along in a ludicrous fashion. (On holiday in Ireland

Robin with Ben as a new baby, February, 1974
James Ravilious

in 1976, we had village children in stitches at the sight of it.) The Robin was our only first-hand car, and it did us proud until James began to need to transport framed exhibitions, and other large freight. Then, at last, he took a normal driving test, passing it with ease, so that we could begin on a series of undistinguished second-hand hatchbacks. He enjoyed driving, and was good at it. He was fast but courteous, and had very swift reactions. He also had a remarkable talent for reversing. Perhaps it was an acute spatial awareness; at any rate, he could drive backwards as easily as forwards, and at much the same speed – a useful skill in our narrow lanes.

In 1977 he acquired a part-time assistant, George Tucker. James was always helpful and understanding to the young and diffident: shy girls self-conscious about their looks, and students, like George, at the start of their careers. A native Devonian, son of a line of agricultural engineers in Hatherleigh, George had done a photography A Level in Exeter, and at twenty was recommended to James by a mutual friend when he began to need an assistant. George did basic darkroom work for him and helped with setting up exhibitions. Eventually, James encouraged him to do a Photography BA at Derby, though George said later that he learnt more from working for James than from all his official studies. He has remained a devoted disciple, taking his own excellent photos to record his home countryside, and elsewhere, in the style of James's work.

In 1975, the Dolton branch of the Women's Institute got wind of what James was doing and invited him to one of their monthly meetings as guest speaker. His duties were to give a short talk after the committee proceedings, with slides of his work, and then judge the competition of the month. This happened to be on the theme of Most Interesting Old Photo. Judging it, and talking to the members, James realised that there was an untapped source of early photographs in old family albums and shoeboxes all over the district: fascinating pictures of the same places that he was recording, but taken in the very early 1900s, sometimes earlier. In those days, before the arrival of the ubiquitous Box Brownie camera, such photos were often well-taken by trained photographers (the local chemist or shopkeeper adding a second source of income). But the prints that came to light were getting dog-eared and beginning to fade; and most were unlabelled. Their current owners could perhaps identify places and people in them, but memories would soon fade like the prints. James couldn't bear to think of such rich and diverse documentation being thrown away. He persuaded the Beaford Centre that the old prints ought to be copied, and their known details recorded, as an important other strand of his work. It came to be known as the Old Archive. He bought the equipment to do it himself, and built a portable copy-stand to hold a camera and lights for the work, later donating them to the archive. In the end, he copied about five thousand photos, but after that he felt he had neither pay nor time for this as well as his own photography. George Tucker, followed by other colleagues – Beryl Yates, Bryony Harris and Liz Taynton – carried on the Old Archive work, adding another three thousand images, and dealing with exhibitions, publications and research. All these images are available now online.

The Old Archive (once immortalised in the *Farmers' Weekly* as 'Fadographs of Yestern Scenes') includes photos of school line-ups and outings, special occasions, fancy dress, village scenes, everyday dress, transport, trades and shops, and a certain amount of farming. They show the communities James was working in as they had been two or three generations further back. Often buildings and families, occasionally even individual people, crop up in both collections. The old pictures are, of necessity, more static, more posed, because of the length of exposure required by the early cameras, and they are seldom of interiors, owing to the problems of lighting them, but they can still be absorbing. Even the school photos, when viewed in succession, reveal a lot about the changes in school life and the children's attitudes. The scared and

rigid rows in snowy pinafores, cut-down jackets and boots turn gradually into relaxed and smiling groups in short, casual clothes. Some of the pictures anticipate enormous change to come. In Dolton, for instance, the Old Archive documented the arrival of the first car in the village – the doctor's new Wolseley – which drew a crowd there c. 1910. Seventy-five years later James recorded the primary school's first computer.

It is fascinating to compare the two collections. James mounted a revealing little exhibition in 1976 called *Then and Now*, for which he specifically retook some of the old places for comparison. But to us it was a rather melancholy task. In the intervening years old vernacular buildings had been modernised out of all recognition: the deep thatched roofs slated at an uglier,

Alleyway at Landkey, c. 1900
Beaford Archives

Alleyway at Landkey, 1975
James Ravilious/Beaford Archive

shallower angle; the old small-paned windows replaced by disproportionate modern ones. Some venerable buildings were melting back into the soil from which they came; others had been completely bulldozed from the scene; while most village streets had been weeded and surfaced and filled with signs and cars and lights and aerials. The neatness, the sharpened angles, the dominance of the car, all combined to make these places less appealing visually. We did acknowledge, however, that the life lived in them was a great deal more comfortable in our day than in the early 1900s. People who talked to us about life back then were always torn between regrets for the past, and wonder at the privations and sheer hard work they had endured.

On the other hand, the photos of home-grown communal celebrations for national events, and of carnivals and fairs, demonstrate an extraordinary continuity. The love of decoration, of dressing up and losing inhibitions, and the competitive creativity that all this brought out in people, were still just as strong in James's time as they had been seventy years earlier. (They are still in evidence today.) At the turn of the century, people had dressed the streets with arches of greenery and flags to mark the Relief of Mafeking, and created horse-drawn carnival floats featuring John Bull and Britannia, with patriotic titles such as 'England's Pride and Glory'. In James's day, they put up flags and bunting once again and made giant cakes for the Queen's Silver Jubilee, and based their fancy dress costumes on news items or television soaps. The humour had got a good deal broader over the years, especially on the Young Farmers' floats, but the massive village teas, the folk art spirit, and the work put into decorating trailers, which were often still completely covered in hand-made crêpe-paper work, continued with the same inventiveness and energy.

For James, these two strands of his work fed each other. In the 1970s so many people were related to each other all across the area that there was a network of connections for him to follow up. While making his own record, he would get to hear about old photos to copy; in carrying out the copying he would get talking to new people, and be invited into fascinating interiors. Studying the old photos, both the content that made them interesting seventy years later, and what was tantalisingly missing, gave him insights into what he himself should be recording for the future. Also it impressed on him the need for data to go with each picture. For too many of the old photos, the current owner could offer no details except the village where they were taken. James saw at first hand how much dates and names and other facts enhanced a photograph down the years. Difficult as it was to do both simultaneously, he made as many notes as he could while he

was doing the copying (usually on someone's kitchen table while she plied him with tea and talk). Soon he was giving slide-shows all over the district, adapting the selection to each place, and collecting more material and information as he went. At many of the venues the comments and reminiscences which greeted each slide would swell to an enthusiastic roar.

In those early days, exhibitions were the main way to display the archive to a wider audience so, as the pages of negatives began to mount up, James showed prints from both archives on the wall of the Music Room at the Beaford Centre. His work was spotted by Andrew Jewell, Keeper of the

Woman in fancy dress as Britannia, Dolton, c. 1910
Beaford Archives

Young men in fancy dress, Winkleigh Fair, 1982
James Ravilious/Beaford Archive

Museum of English Rural Life at Reading University. Andrew came from a rural Cornish background; he appreciated what James was doing. He gave him his first prestigious exhibition, entitled *The View from Beaford*, at Reading Museum in 1973. After this there were other shows: at Southampton University, in Brittany, in other venues in London, and throughout the West Country. In 1980 he was offered an exhibition at the Photographers' Gallery in London, which seemed an exciting step forward. It got a nice mention on *Kaleidoscope*, the BBC radio arts magazine, and William Packer wrote in the *Financial Times*: 'He looks out upon a community, and the countryside that has formed it, with a quiet and loving understanding, celebrating the enviable certainty and normality of the country routine and the turn of the year, its covert dramas and modest triumphs.'

But although such shows were well received, and produced some print sales, they seldom led on to anything much. James didn't really know how to capitalise on such things by 'networking'. Also, his attention would move on to something else. In any case, exhibitions were expensive in money and time. Only the local ones received any backing through the Beaford Centre.

Meanwhile, he was mounting a number of displays on portable stands in other local venues. These were usually supported by Beaford (though, typically, James seldom kept within his budget, and therefore paid for a good deal himself). One very enjoyable one was an exhibition we worked on together at the invitation of the primary school in the small market town of Hatherleigh to celebrate the centenary of its building. Hatherleigh was particularly rich in early photos, which James had copied for the Old Archive. These we exhibited enlarged and mounted on big free-standing screens. We also went round meeting former pupils from the early 1900s, collecting stories and schoolwork which they had preserved in order to make an additional display of related objects. Piercing an eyehole through one of the screens, we constructed a little peepshow of an Edwardian child's bedroom containing contemporary toys and schoolwork – workbooks in beautiful copperplate handwriting, writing slates and pieces of handywork – with a life-size model of the supposed owner of the room, looking out of a *trompe l'oeil* window at a much-enlarged old photo of the main street of Hatherleigh full of Edwardian crowds. In collecting for the display, we met old men who, at the age of six, had ridden their ponies two or three miles to school every day in all weathers, with only a baked potato in their pockets for lunch, and then ridden home in the afternoon to do their share of tasks on the farm; and we talked to elderly ladies who had been part of the same group of friends and neighbours ever since they started at the school before the age of five.

As the two collections grew, we began to hope for a permanent North Devon venue for displaying quality prints of them both – a showcase for James's work and for the old photographs – and also for visiting shows of photography or anything else related to local life, such as historic farm implements, for instance, or traditional crafts. In James's hopes, it featured safe storage for his negatives, a darkroom where the day-to-day work could be processed, a workshop for preparing exhibitions, a study area where academic work could enrich the collection and, most important, an adequate exhibition space. He saw it as a 'destination' where locals and visitors could see North Devon (and indeed country life in general) celebrated. We had been to Yorkshire and seen how Frank Meadow Sutcliffe's photographs of everyday life in Whitby at the end of the nineteenth century had become a valued feature there.

We wrote our first short proposal, and from then on the powers that be blew hot and cold on the project for nearly fifteen years as successive administrations at Beaford took up the idea, and then dropped it again because the financial tide had turned, or staff had moved on. We continued to keep an eye open on our travels for a suitable building, and at one time there was what seemed to be quite a promising possibility that the two old stone barns behind the Beaford Centre itself might be converted for the project. That even got as far as architect's drawings (though no one thought to consult James when they were being made). But then, to his deep disappointment, it all returned to the back burner once again. It was too big a scheme financially, and too much distraction from the Beaford Centre's perceived purposes. Raising the funds in the first place, and then running a venue, were not the sort of things they could contemplate. With hindsight, of course, if such a plan had been developed, the recession would probably have killed it off.

14 . THE BEAFORD CENTRE

JAMES'S RELATIONSHIP WITH the Beaford Centre was not a very happy one after John Lane moved on. His annual salary fluctuated, but was hardly generous. Whether full-time or part-time, it never reached the equivalent of £11,000 in today's values. Without my grandfather's gift of the cottage we couldn't possibly have lived on it for long. But low pay would not have bothered James much if he had felt that his work was valued and promoted. It was not easy for a solo artist like him to work for an administration whose staff, finances and policies were in constant flux; or to be dictated to by people who knew less about the visual arts than he did. His task was defined so vaguely, and did not produce appreciable 'outcomes', or generate the kind of income for the Centre which might have better justified his salary in official eyes. His many exhibitions beyond North Devon were seldom, if ever, seen by Beaford Centre staff. Nor were the slide-shows he presented to visiting groups and schools, often in the room directly below the staff offices. From time to time he was required to put up some of his photos in the Music Room and corridors to entertain those schools or to impress dignitaries, but in general his work seems hardly to have been viewed as integral to the organisation at all. Directors came and went throughout his time there. Some liked his work but could find few funds to support it. Some were indifferent, or had other agendas. One resented supporting the archive at all and called it a 'white elephant'.

An irritant for James was Beaford's requirement that he take publicity shots of its performance events: work which was taxing and thankless to do. Most of the results have apparently disappeared. A second condition was that he would provide a large number of reference prints of his best work for staff to use to demonstrate the archive, and to generate reproduction income for the centre's funds. James reluctantly undertook to do this in 1984, but dragged his feet for several years for two reasons: he didn't feel confident that his work would be used respectfully; and experience had taught him that the prints would not be carefully preserved. Ten years after his death there was no one left on the Beaford staff who even knew of those prints' existence till I mentioned them, and they were eventually found.

Admittedly, James was not an ideal employee. He was too forgetful to keep records; he chafed at the time wasted at staff meetings which didn't concern him; and he resented the constraints of administrative regulations. He was by temperament a solo flier – though he certainly enjoyed collaboration with someone he respected.

Probably, like his father, he gave a misleadingly laid-back impression. The genial, modest chap lounging around at coffee-time, entertaining fellow staff with anecdotes, or sharing their moans about the management, may not have seemed much like a dedicated artist. They would not have known that he had been out at work since 6 a.m., or that he might be in the darkroom later until after midnight. I doubt if any of them thought then that he would make a name for himself, and Beaford. On the other hand, he probably underestimated the constant time-consuming search for public funding that arts organisations have to keep up – funding which is more often available for innovation than maintenance of an ongoing project – and which became harder and harder to find in the 1980s for support of a single artist's work. The dual nature of his archive, both social history and an artist's oeuvre, was always a complication. Funding bodies for the two aspects had quite different criteria, and tended only to support one or the other.

In his modest way, James came to feel that he had dedicated himself to creating something of lasting value to the community, a value that would increase with time. He also saw his work as an ambassador for the Beaford Centre and for North Devon. But it seemed to him that his employers viewed it more as *his* career, *his* self-promotion, an anomaly among their projects, so that they begrudged the continual hunt for funding for it year after year. He longed to establish the archive as part of a vibrant enterprise celebrating our special bit of country, but instead he often felt his work was undervalued, ignored, or downright snubbed. In bad patches that hurt a great deal.

James didn't have the ego to stand up to this. Nervousness made him rather incoherent, so he dreaded confrontations and gave a poor account of himself at meetings as a result. Nor could he sell himself. It simply wasn't in his nature to point out the value of his work to the unseeing. Outside the Beaford Centre, in the locality and in more metropolitan circles, people were saying that the archive was the best project Beaford had instigated. It has certainly proved to be by far the longest-lasting. But the management, dependent as it was on precarious public funding, would not, or could not, recognise this. When funds became scarcer, he was reduced to part-time hours. In theory, this meant that he could do more freelance work as well, which he did. But his heart and soul were in the archive and he tended to go on working at it, paid or not, unless temporarily paralysed by depression.

15 . THE MIDDLE YEARS

HOWEVER, FUNDING, SUCH AS IT WAS, did keep coming for over seventeen years, and that length of employment gave James a luxury few other documentary photographers enjoy: time. Time to immerse himself in the place and its way of life; time to explore every lane; and time to return again and again to a scene, or a happening, and to go on taking it until he got the shots he wanted. This he did a number of times with the annual Walk of the Iddesleigh Friendly Society which still takes place every May. Only two villages near us kept up this custom, though many had had such clubs before the war. They had been formed in the nineteenth century as self-help organisations in the days when there was no other safety net for agricultural labourers if they were unwell, if work was scarce, or if times were hard in other ways. By paying a small subscription into a village fund, they could insure against such times, and get a bit of financial help when they needed it. The clubs' importance waned when National Insurance and the welfare state came in, but a few communities were reluctant to give up their own special annual day; and even members who had moved some distance away would return to be part of the 'Club Day' festivities.

At Iddesleigh on Club Day, the members gather for a church service, and then a drink in the pub, before processing down to the village hall (formerly the school) for lunch and club business. In the afternoon they put on a sports day for the children, followed by a dance. This home-grown event, in a tiny, very traditional village, gave James the chance to record something like a mediaeval painting: a whole village taking a day off to enjoy itself. The procession, with band and banner, which escorted the casseroles of hot mashed potato from the pub down to the village hall for the members' lunch was a scene not unlike the country wedding, with its bagpipe players and trays of broth, which Pieter Breughel the Elder painted in Brussels in around 1568.

North Devonians always seem to welcome special occasions, religious, patriotic or secular. The Old Archive is full of photos of events: processions for the Sunday schools of different denominations, club walks, fêtes for innumerable good causes and vast teas for the entire populace to celebrate public events. People have been dressing up, decorating their streets and houses, creating elaborate floats and parading with bands for royal milestones, national events and holy days since at least Victorian times. They still love the excuse for another jollity.

For James, these cheerful happenings offered a lively contrast to the more serious subject of farming, and he made the most of them. In the summer months, there were traditional fairs at Torrington, Winkleigh and Chulmleigh which he often covered, enjoying the crowds, and the fancy dress particularly. In the autumn he attended Hatherleigh's carnival in eight different years, and Dolton's in eleven, relishing the creativity they brought out in people, and the excitement of crowded streets and burning torches in the dark of a November night.

Hatherleigh's Ascension Day Sunday School parade with its silver band and 'garland', crossed hoops dressed with flowers held aloft on a pole, was another lure. So were flower shows. As always, he liked to record the prepara-

Top: Friendly Society parade, with mashed potato, Iddesleigh, 1975
James Ravilious/Beaford Archive
Below: *The Peasants' Wedding*, c. 1568 (oil) by Pieter Breughel the Elder
Kuntshistorisches Museum, Vienna

tions for these: the secret grooming of trays of vegetables and flower arrangements, and the intent little huddles of judges about to make someone's day – or dash their hopes.

Less frequent, but just as rewarding, were the royal occasions. There are three coronations and three jubilees acknowledged with patriotic enthusiasm in the old photographs, and James was eager to carry on that tradition. In 1977 he travelled all over his territory taking shop windows, private houses, churches and chapels, even our local postbox, decorated in preparation for the Queen's Silver Jubilee. On 6 June, having done his research beforehand, he dashed from village to village recording an acreage of loaded tea tables, as well as dancing and the presentation of commemorative mugs to the children, in Dolton, Burrington, High Bickington and Atherington, taking some of it in colour,

Jack Mardon decorating his house
for the Queen's Jubilee, Dolton, 1977
James Ravilious/Beaford Archive

too. Four years later, on Charles and Diana's wedding day in July 1981, more festivities occurred, and more mugs were presented. James was in Iddesleigh for these, but he also found time to take the television presentation being watched on a big screen in Dolton village hall, and to nip over to Ashreigney and up the church tower in order to take that whole village assembled for its big day.

There were also quieter scenes to revisit. James had a regular appointment with the bluebells which pour down our steep little wood, Rushleigh Copse. At about 5 p.m. on an early May evening the descending sun shines in at the top of the wood casting long soft rays all the way down through the trees, lighting a feathery cascade of flowers and ferns in their path, reminding him of a Samuel Palmer. Year after year James would be there at the bottom

Bluebells in Rushleigh Copse,
Addisford, Dolton, c. 1985
James Ravilious

The Herdsman's Cottage, 1850 (etching) by Samuel Palmer
Private collection

of the slope, breathing in the drowsy perfumed air, and waiting for the five minutes or so when those rays were at their best. It was a difficult scene to compose, and he took it many times, in different formats, never quite satisfied.

As he went about his territory he was able to note other likely scenes and return when the light, or the season, or some activity would be right for a shot; working like a cinematographer in a sense, identifying settings for some action in advance – or at least as much in advance as real life allows. So he would take note of the collection times on a post box in an attractive setting, and go back months later to catch a postman picking up the mail. Or he would spot a doorway in an old cob wall with intriguing shadows, and plan to return when someone might be going through it. He liked the unconventional view-point from church towers, and got permission to climb several. There he would

Churchyard steps, Winkleigh, 1982
James Ravilious/Beaford Archive

Running for the school bus,
Atherington, 1982
James Ravilious/Beaford Archive

brave the cold as he waited for something interesting to happen below – a schoolboy running for his bus, perhaps, past the gravestones of the village forefathers, or the tower's shadow reaching out across a field of corn. There were many times when we passed a gateway or an alley which he saw as a good composition and he would say he must come back for that in evening light when the shadows would fall best, or at a winter dawn when the trees would be bare, or when the view was under snow. It was one of the great benefits of the job that he could do this. 'I'm always returning to places,' he said. 'I don't have pressure of time. I can go back ten years later.'

He told an interviewer, 'I see places as super locations and think: when will there be some actors?' 'I like the idea of a landscape with humanity in it.' His 'actors' were not always human. Many were animals: sheep, cows or horses; a cat pouncing in a hedge; a dog wandering down a lane; or even just a trio of swifts sketching a joyful flourish over an empty street. Like the landscape painters of old, he felt a scene needed that little bit of animation. He would wait for it literally for hours sometimes, on a windy hilltop, or the draughty corner of a street.

Meanwhile, some good projects were afoot which were not connected to Beaford at all; he was getting involved in books. Usually, when he was out and about alone, James would ring in from time to time if he found a phone box handy. One morning he rang from the box on the Green at Iddesleigh to say he had met a couple of interesting schoolteachers who were moving to the village, and he was going to have coffee with them there in the fine old cob-and-thatch pub, the Duke of York. He would be home shortly, he said. A couple of hours later he rang again to say he was still talking to the couple, was going to have lunch with them, and might not be back for some time. The couple were Clare and Michael Morpurgo who were there to set up their groundbreaking charity, Farms For City Children, at Nethercott, a Victorian mansion near the village. Like me, Clare had spent magical holidays as a child in this bit of countryside. Our friendship with her and Michael led to a collaboration in 1978/9 on one of Michael's early books, a diary of a year's work on nearby Parsonage Farm, the farm which gives visiting children from deprived urban areas their first taste of country life, and eye-opening hands-on experience of farmwork. Called *All Around the Year*, the book included poems specially written by Ted Hughes, a friend of the Morpurgos, and photographs by James recording the annual round of life at Parsonage, plus some little decorations of mine. Apart from the fun of the collaboration, James saw it as a valuable project which would give him new insight into the farming world, and photo opportunities he might otherwise have missed. Though the pictures he took had been paid for by Michael, he put them into the archive.

But there were hard times too. At Christmas 1977, I discovered I was pregnant again. It was not an easy pregnancy this time. My father's collapsing marriage, and Theresa's consequent move to Dolton in a state of breakdown, dominated it from the start, bringing me constant stress. By eight and a half months I was physically and emotionally worn out. Suddenly, one afternoon, the normally energetic baby ceased to kick. After two days of waiting, and checks at health centre and hospital, the gynaecologists confirmed that it was dead. For some reason I never understood, they advised against inducing the birth and sent me away 'to wait for nature to take its course'. I went home and waited. As day after day went by, the grief and feeling of waste were compounded with a growing sense of horror at what I was carrying. Eventually, after ten long days, nature rescued me. I went back to hospital for the strange charade of a birth, and home again to cope with unneeded milk and a flood of useless mothering hormones – a physical craving for something to hug. James was there to be hugged whenever I needed him – a gentle, sympathetic and patient rock throughout. He went alone to Barnstaple to bury our daughter in a tiny white box. I'm ashamed to say I don't know how much it affected him. I was too inward-turned, and concentrating hard on trying to hold things together for four-year-old Ben.

After my six-week check-up James suggested a holiday, perhaps in France. I found the smallest decision almost impossible at the time, but managed to agree at last if it were my favourite country Italy instead, though the thought of leaving Ben seemed unbearable. James gently pushed me into it, and organised everything. In the train to Heathrow I was quietly dripping tears for most of the way, somehow convinced that I would never see Ben again. James protested with a gentle 'Dar-ling!' at my uncharacteristic lack of reserve.

Priest in cloisters, San Gimignano, Italy, 1978
James Ravilious

Italy was as warm and welcoming as ever, even in October, and had a healing effect. And it was all new territory to James. We travelled by train or bus, wandering at will, staying in Pisa, Perugia, Siena and San Gimignano, a place which had lived in my memory like a heavenly citadel ever since I had last seen it at the age of fourteen silhouetted against an apricot sky. There we explored the enchanting little hilltop town, and then, to get a distant view of its crown of towers, scrambled down through the olive groves and up to a small farm where we did our halting best to chat up the farmer and his wife. Soon the trip turned into a Piero della Francesca pilgrimage, for James particularly loved Piero's grave, monumental figures. We visited Arrezzo and Sansepolcro, and took a vertiginous bus trip over the mountains to Urbino. He was thrilled by the reminders of Renaissance paintings that we saw at every turn in the streets and countryside. When he wasn't worshipping at Piero's shrines, he was loitering in alleys and watching at doorways, recording people and their everyday lives.

Soon after the publication of *All Around the Year,* James got a letter from an editor with Scolar Press, a small London publishing house, who said how much she had enjoyed his recent exhibition at the Serpentine Gallery, and that she would like to talk to him about his work. Her name was Helen Dore, and she was prepared to trek all the way to Addisford to meet him.

We didn't know any editors then, and were surprised by the woman who arrived at our door. Her accent and dress (headscarf, tweed skirt and sensible shoes) were those of a well-born English country lady. It was only when we took in the striking tawny eyes that she had inherited from her Armenian father that we realised how un-English she was. James showed her piles of photos, which she admired. Then we drove her about to show her the actual sites and she fell in love with our environment. So the idea of a book was born. The collaboration was to be exciting and nerve-racking in equal measure. Helen became a generous and supportive friend, involving herself in our family life, and enduring many less-than-comfortable nights on the camp bed in our kitchen.

James led the picture selection for the book, making primarily visual choices, and covering every surface in the sitting room with reference prints so as to choose pairings of images, and the rhythm of the whole sequence; he had very high standards for the presentation of books or exhibitions. With my growing interest in local history, I chose more by content, so sometimes we had to compromise.

When it came to finding someone to write an accompanying text, he proposed me. (He used to call me 'the brains of the partnership'.) I had no similar work to my name, except that three years earlier I had won the *Sunday Times*'s Kenneth Allsop memorial essay competition with a piece on the importance of hedges and their upkeep, which I had based on a year's study of the flora and fauna in an ancient hedge of our own. Helen approved and, nervously, I began to write the various section introductions. Then, when the picture choices were agreed, I wrote their captions using the factual information James had collected or I had researched, but with an interpretation of my own. Sometimes I could articulate his reasons for taking a certain picture, which he had not been conscious of when he took it. I felt our roles were the reverse of normal book-writing, where the photographs illustrate the text. Here, the photos were paramount, and the purpose of the words to add any dimension that couldn't be visually conveyed.

We asked Ronald Blythe, author of that classic record of Norfolk village life, *Akenfield,* to write an introduction. Though we didn't know him personally, he had been a close friend of John and Christine Nash, and was also a friend of my father, having acquired one of his engraved glasses. When Ronald saw an advance proof of the book he wrote to us: 'what I particularly loved about it was the way it was controlled by the discipline of "recording". You are seeing the actual, the *Now*, and through the most seeing of eyes.'

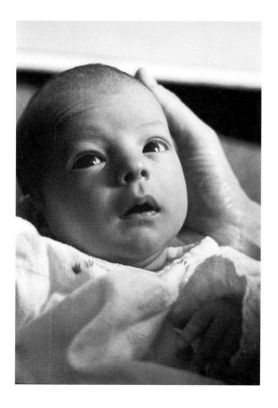

It was an anxious time. James was naturally very nervous about the book, and I suffered intermittently from new writer's block. Also I was pregnant again and, with the previous disaster in mind, the doctors were making much more fuss of me than before. Helen was a long-suffering editor. Summoned to hospital a month in advance of my due date, I had to dictate my last sentence to her, just before the print deadline, over the phone from my hospital bed. But all went well. Ella was induced three weeks early, arriving without incident, a small but serene little image in perfect health. And the

Ella Ravilious, five days old, February, 1980
James Ravilious

book, *The Heart of the Country*, when it reached us, was finely designed and printed. James was not yet at his peak technically, so the photography was less subtle than would satisfy him later on, but at the time he was pleased.

Reviewers were enthusiastic. In *The Guardian*, William Trevor wrote that the book 'charts magnificently the secluded world in which the rivers Torridge and Taw dictate the lie of the land . . . This is a remarkable book, its photographs juicy with atmosphere.' Bruce Bernard, picture editor at the *Sunday Times*, wrote: 'What is exceptional about James Ravilious is the sense of deep familiarity with, and knowledge of, his subject. The pictures impart a feeling of the very particular actuality of each scene in a way that I have never seen before with photography of this kind. . . . A moving and memorable document.'

The Scolar Press launched the book with a party at Beaford, to which we invited most of the people in the photographs. Many came, including some of James's stars such as Archie Parkhouse and Olive Bennett, in their Sunday best and enjoying their celebrity. Few, if any, had ever set foot in the Beaford Centre before.

Another highlight of that period was the trip James made to France with a friend, Tony Foster. They had met when Tony, as a Visual Arts Officer at South West Arts, the local branch of the Arts Council, was largely responsible for recommending grants to Beaford for the support of James's work. Tony was one of the first officials to see his worth, and has fought his corner most faithfully ever since. Tony left SWA in the early 1980s to become a watercolour landscape painter. We had been friends for some time when, in 1981, he suggested that he and James should go on a working trip together. The ultimate goal was a walk through the Cévennes in the steps of R. L. Stevenson (described in his delightful book, *Travels with a Donkey in the Cévennes,* 1879) but they prudently made several practice runs in Cornwall, and one in Wales, to see if their working modes were compatible.

Tony was a tougher and more professional camper than James, even then. Later he would walk the world's wildernesses, often alone for days, painting huge watercolour landscapes in extraordinary detail, and surviving on bread and raw onions, in desert heat or snow. But the early projects were modest enough for James to enjoy, once he'd stopped moaning about his blisters. They found their work patterns fitted together well. Tony would select a suitable spot for a painting and settle down to work, while James explored ahead, camera in hand.

Towards evening when the light began to change, Tony would catch him up so that they could share their day's experiences, eat together, and either set up camp or find lodging for the night. They laughed a lot, and encouraged each other.

Tony recounts an incident on one of the trial excursions. He was painting a view overlooking Fowey near his home in Cornwall while James sat nearby waiting for him to finish, when that bane of outdoor painters, a nosy bystander, turned up and peered over Tony's shoulder to watch him work.

'Are you amateur or professional?' he enquired after a while.

'Well,' replied Tony modestly, 'professional, I suppose.'

'What name do you paint under?'

At once James put in helpfully, 'His nom de brush is Newton Winsor.'

'Oh,' said the man, satisfied. 'I think I've heard of you. You're quite well known, aren't you?'

The Cévennes trip, in the spring of 1982, was hugely rewarding. Dissuaded by me from using an actual donkey (which would probably have given them as much trouble as Modéstine gave Stevenson), they loaded their gear on a golf-trolley, a much more tractable beast of burden. They expected a lush French April, but up in the mountains it was still pretty wintry. There was even snow on the bleak limestone crags of Mont Lozère. Camping was not too attractive in those conditions so, like Stevenson, they often cadged

Top: Men playing boules, Le Monastier, Cévennes, France, 1982
James Ravilious
Below: Riders in a tree-lined street, Florac, Cévennes, France 1982
James Ravilious

shelter from an obliging farmer. Settling down for a noisy night in a hayloft over a barnful of sheep, after a supper of wine and porridge, James observed, 'At last I feel I'm above the common herd.'

But spring was getting going in the valleys, especially around La Vernède, a magical district of primitive granite farms and blossoming almond trees surrounded by hills that were completely clothed in ancient sweet chestnut forest. Despite the challenging conditions, James was on fire. He took more of his best images than in any other three-week period of his career.

France was always a lure. From time to time, when he felt in need of refreshment, James would take off on his motorbike alone for a long weekend there. In 1977 he returned to the area near Rouen where he had stayed with the Swanzys in his student days, rediscovering Les Andelys, and the romantic ruins of the twelfth-century Abbaye de Fontaine-Guérard, which he particu-

Ruined abbey, Jumièges, France, c. 1986
James Ravilious

larly loved, before wandering on up the Seine. On later visits he explored elsewhere in Normandy, and along the Loire. The pictures he took are a mix of architecture, such as Jumièges Abbey and the seventeenth-century dovecot at Mortemer, and everyday life in the villages he passed.

He accepted occasional commissions that took him afield in Britain, to the Lake District, for instance, and to work with Christopher Milne on illustrations for his books, and with Frank Delaney on a book about John Betjeman (which included a portrait of Betjeman in old age). In 1986 he covered a four-month multi-cultural festival of the arts initiated by the writer John Moat for the organisation Concord. Directed by Cy Grant, this charitable trust had been running such festivals to celebrate world culture in cities and towns throughout the UK. For the Concord in Devon project James recorded Ghanaian drummers, Ukrainian and Kathak Indian dancers, Japanese No players, a Peruvian panpipe band, West Indian steel bands and Chinese flautists, performing and holding workshops in schools and halls all over the county, as well as an inter-faith vigil for peace in Exeter Cathedral.

He was also commissioned to do portrait work from time to time, by the Orchard Theatre actors, the Dartington Hall Trustees, the staff of South West Arts and the Alberni Quartet, among others and, for the *Sunday Times*'s picture editor, one or two portraits of West Country artists such as Patrick Heron. He found formal portrait work a bit of a strain; but I can testify that it was much easier to be photographed by James than by other photographers because he was so quick and seemingly casual that one didn't have time to stiffen up.

16 . DARKROOM

JAMES COULD SELDOM BEAR TO WAIT long to examine his catch, so after a day's shooting, and a pause for food, he would usually disappear into the darkroom to begin the laborious process of discovery.

A darkroom was a very private world in his day (behind a locked door, usually, in case an intruder ruined light-sensitive film or paper by entering without a warning knock). Few non-photographers knew what went on in them. Nowadays, even photographers don't always know. Since James spent so much of his life in there, it is perhaps worth describing in detail what he did.

Photographic film is highly sensitive to light until fixed by chemical processes. So until that point James had to handle it in pitch darkness. Immured in a small blacked-out cupboard of a room, he would take out the day's film rolls and coil them in a tank of developer. This had to be gently inverted twice a minute for ten minutes. Then other chemicals, first acid stop bath for thirty seconds, then fixative for five minutes, replaced the developer. This fixed the images so light could no longer alter them. This stage of the process left him with long strips of about thirty-six 24mm × 36mm 'negative' images – that is, images in which the dark and light elements of the original scene are reversed so that a dark tree silhouetted against snow would appear on the film as a white tree against a dark ground. These are hard to read until one gets used to it. Finally, the films were washed in running water for thirty minutes before being hung up to dry for several hours, or overnight.

At the next session, the lengths of developed film had first to be carefully cut into short strips of six images each. Then three large trays containing pungent chemicals mixed at precise dilutions and temperature had to be prepared. In the satanic red glow of a 'safe' light, James assembled the strips of negatives on the desk, six rows at a time, on a piece of white-light-sensitive paper in a special frame he had made, and held them down with a sheet of clear glass. Over them, the enlarger, a lens with a bright light above it attached to a column, was then switched on for ten seconds to reverse the negative images into positives on the paper, creating the 'contact sheet'. Back in dim red light, the paper (still blank in appearance) went into the developer tray to be tossed and stirred for a controlled length of time till, as the chemicals worked their magic on the paper's silver gelatin, the grid of thirty-six images slowly dawned. Then the sheet was moved on through the other trays for the developing process to be stopped, the images fixed, and the surplus chemicals washed off. Only when that contact sheet had reached the third tray could James return to ordinary light; and only when the sheet was hung from an overhead string to dry could he really begin to assess the tiny photographs on it with the help of a magnifier. He went through this whole process some 2,300 times just to make contact sheets of his archive work alone. There are many, many more of his private photographs.

But the contact sheets were only the beginning. The next stage was to make reference prints of any of the images that looked hopeful. For this, the relevant strip of film was fed into the enlarger so as to isolate a single negative image. By sliding the lens up or down its column an enlarged positive of that image would be projected on to the white desktop below and focused there within a 10" × 8" frame. With the safe light on, a piece of light-sensitive resin-coated paper was slipped into place, and the enlarger light turned on again for a short burst. This paper, like the contact sheets, had to make a timed progress through the various baths and be washed and dried before final assessment. The reference prints, literally thousands of them, were James's main tool for all future uses such as selecting for publication and exhibition, and as guidance for making bigger prints. In those pre-scanning days, they were also sent out to publishers for reproduction.

Printing for exhibitions or sale was the final, most demanding, stage. Now the paper would be fibre-based and much larger – from 9" × 12" up to an unwieldy 20" × 24" – and because of its quality and size, very much more expensive. At this point artistic skill came back into play, timing of the exposure to the light being absolutely critical; though, with experience, he became adept at judging this.

Some negatives required 'burning in' or 'dodging': manipulation of the image by exposing parts of it half a second more, or less, than the rest, so that they received slightly more or less light – necessary, for example, for skies, or with a figure silhouetted against snow, or a bright window in a dark interior. This could involve hovering over a part of the projected image with his hand, or with a homemade 'mask', a piece of card with a hole or a profile specially cut to correspond with the relevant part of the image. Most negatives needed some sort of tweak to be seen at their best. It was far more time-consuming than most people realised, thinking, as they often did, that a print could be 'run off' like a photocopy.

The whole process seemed to me a bit like elaborate cookery, but done mainly in the half-dark, dabbling in nasty liquids in an evil-smelling kitchen, with no guarantee that the resulting dish would be satisfactory; and working to recipes which varied with each image, with each different brand of chemical and paper, and even with different atmospheric conditions. The perfect result could only be achieved by trial and error on test strips and wasted sheets of paper – each of which must go through the whole sequence before it could be judged.

In those days photography was perhaps unique among the visual arts in the degree to which the final result was an act of faith on the part of its creator. Other printing techniques involve the artist in a certain amount of suspense. The wood engraver cannot really know what he has achieved till a print lies glistening before him, but at least he has some leeway to go back and tinker with his block to improve it. A metal engraver, or etcher, such as Samuel Palmer, could re-work his plates many times to refine his miraculous soft light effects with extra hatching. But those artists could *see* what they were working on, even though it was obscure, and in reverse. The traditional photographer worked with a double dose of suspense. The image he hoped he had taken was invisible in the camera till he could develop the film; and then the print he made of it could not be fully assessed until it had been through all these processes. The moment he had tried to capture was usually unrepeatable.

Not by nature a patient man, James willingly spent hour upon hour of painstaking work in the darkroom – as any pre-digital photographer had to do, of course, unless he was rich enough to pay an assistant or a studio to do it for him. To me, occasionally roped in to help with moving on the prints through the trays of chemicals, darkroom work seemed the tedious and unpleasant part of the job. But when it went well James enjoyed the craft of it; and he became increasingly skilled at judging negatives and timings by eye. If negatives or prints were unsatisfactory he was frustrated and cast down. His kind of photography took a mix of quite contrasting attributes: patience but very quick reactions in the field; and artistic skill coupled with a meticulous scientific approach in the darkroom afterwards.

17 . THE MAN BEHIND THE CAMERA

JAMES WAS A MAN OF CONTRASTS: artistic yet scientific; impulsive and highly strung but endlessly patient over his work; responsive to people and beauty but unable to express himself easily in words; sociable and funny, but at times depressed; hopeful that his work was of value, but needing affirmation to boost his confidence.

To me, his most important quality was his honesty in everything he was, and did. He was straight with people, and assumed that they would be with him – to his cost, at times. On the rare occasions when he disliked or disapproved of someone I could always tell because he was ill at ease with them. He didn't know how to dissemble.

The integrity of his work was paramount. He was making a public document, and he felt a sense of responsibility towards the future. It was important to him that his archive should be as truthful a record of real life going on as he could make it. 'I don't stage-manage a picture,' he said. He never posed his subjects, and he avoided scenarios that he felt had been set up for him to take. For most of the archive work the camera was hand-held, and he wouldn't use artificial lighting, even in the darkest situations. Though he

read Edwin Smith's manual *All the Photo Tricks*, he seldom employed them. His early negatives can be difficult to print, but he tried hard to make later ones as easy to use as possible so that future printers coming after him would be able to produce prints that were faithful to his vision without too much manipulation in the darkroom.

A local reporter once picked up on this point, as James recounted in a speech he made at the launch party for his second book, in 1995. 'Lastly, I will remind you of a trade secret revealed many years ago by the local press. Writing about our first book, *The Heart of the Country*, a journalist revealed that "James rarely tampers with his subjects after he has photographed them." Ladies and gentlemen, there has been a change of policy, and I would now like to tamper with as many of you as possible . . . daughters first, perhaps?'

James at work with Edwin Smith's Ica, Dartmoor, 1996
Chris Chapman

The black line which, following Cartier-Bresson, he created round his prints by exposing a thin rim of paper around the image under the enlarger – and which he insisted on retaining in reproductions – was mainly to protect his careful composition from cropping by ruthless editors and designers; but it was also a statement that the image was the whole truth, as far as he had seen it.

With honesty as his maxim, he could only collaborate with reality – he would never manipulate it. There were many disappointments when he hurried eagerly into the darkroom at the end of a long day only to find, hours later, when a contact sheet came out of the wash, that none of the compositions had quite worked. Other photographers might have cropped down an image in order to 'find' a composition, but James would never do that. He followed Cartier-Bresson's uncompromising rule. In an interview in 1964, Cartier-Bresson said: 'I never crop a photograph. If it needs to be cropped I know it's bad and that nothing could possibly improve it. The only improvement would have been to have taken another picture, at the right place and at the right time.'[6] Similarly, the hoped-for image was irretrievably marred in James's eyes if he had failed to notice a foreign object like a telegraph pole (or, in one instance, his own tripod) in the wrong place. For today's photographers that would present no problems that a swift tickling with Photoshop® could not cure. But for James there were no such dodges or repairs. Either the picture was right in the split second when he pressed the button, or it was not really worth looking at.

Once when they were out and about together, James's brother John, who shared his love of the absurd, asked him admiringly how he managed to find his more surreal subjects. James replied that they were there all around all the time. You just had to be alert for them. He pointed to three elderly ladies with bouffant silver hair-dos sitting in a row on a nearby bench. In the sky above them, as if in mockery, was a line of three little puffs of cloud. 'There you are,' he said. Much as he delighted in technical innovation, I think he would have been wary of digital photography – at least for archival work – because it wasn't necessarily 'honest'. With digital, those three little clouds could have been imported afterwards from another photograph.

James's obsessive streak was not always easy to live with. When he had something on his mind, whether it was work, ill health or employment problems, it dominated his thoughts. When really pushed he could explode briefly, but he was not bad-tempered – far from it. He was too gentle and too modest to throw his weight about.

Like most artists, he needed his work to be acknowledged, but he was not personally ambitious, and did not crave, or expect, fame. In fact, he rather avoided exposure in the local media, because he felt that 'celebrity' would have compromised the naturalness of his relationship with the people that he photographed. He made friends quickly and easily, with men and women of all social levels. They still speak of him lovingly.

In company he did a good deal of the talking, telling amusing anecdotes, making impromptu wordplay, or somewhat *Beano*-type jokes – the sort that were greeted with a laughing groan, 'Oh *James*!' But he was never a show-off – he just seemed to feel it his role to amuse his company. He could fool deliciously in private, too – with an off-the-cuff zaniness that lingers in my mind, even though I can't remember the detail. I can see him now: tall body naked but for socks, perched on the edge of the bed hunting in the rumpled duvet for his other clothes, with a completely spontaneous running commentary on the quest for 'mein Underpantz' in an effortless flow of cod German which could move with ease into Dutch, or a Gaelic lilt, or Peter Sellers Indian.

He relished the absurd. In private, and quite without malice, he rechristened *The Initials in the Heart,* my father's beautiful and poignant book about my mother, as 'The Officials in the Hut'. I ought to have been outraged, but the image was just too funny. And his eye for the surreal led to some ridiculous

shots, usually of animals, which were not quite what his archival brief had called for, but he put them in just for light relief.

In his thirties, he was still boyishly playful. Once at table, when I had won a laughing argument, he grabbed my wrist and forced my hand slowly, inexorably, down into my pudding. Tinned rice and peaches squelched between my fingers as he ordered, 'Say you're sorry! Say you're sorry!'

What made *him* laugh was a gentle, character-led humour – the humour of the old Ealing comedies such as *The Ladykillers* (set in the London he remembered from a happy part of his childhood); and quintessentially English sitcoms such as *Porridge*, *Open All Hours* and *Dad's Army*. For the same reasons he loved Aardman's *Wallace and Gromit* animations. He also had a very soft spot for 'The Fosdyke Saga', Bill Tidy's strip cartoon in the *Daily Mirror*, with its wonderful mix of Northern grit and daft surrealism.

Young bulls eating thistles,
Millhams, Dolton, 1981
James Ravilious/Beaford Archive

He was certainly a talker. He needed to share and talk about his work all the time. If I had not been with him when he took his pictures, he would be eagerly telling me about his day, his catch, as he came in through the door; and making plans to show me what he had discovered. 'You must come and see this beautiful old farm I found. You'll love it!' or 'You have to come and talk to this dear old man I met.' Telephone conversations were audible throughout our cottage so we shared most calls, but later, when we moved to another house and created an office eyrie for him in the roof space with his own phone extension, he would come down two floors after almost every call to report on it.

As each new batch of reference prints emerged from the darkroom and was pegged to dry on the washing line across the sitting room ceiling, he would want my views. If I admired, he was pleased. If I was lukewarm, he would expostulate, 'You bastard! I sweated over three gates and two ploughed fields to get that shot . . . and it's *not* boring!'

On the other hand, he was very self-critical, and particularly wary of being sentimental or trite. He would sometimes condemn one of his pictures that I had liked with, 'Bit of a cliché, isn't it?' or 'No . . . too chocolate-boxy!' In his later catalogue there are occasional comments such as 'Still river, reflected trees. A bit "art", I think.' He was unfashionably modest about his output and would never say it was great. Though I nicknamed his best images 'corkers', he himself would never have called them more than 'quite good . . . I think' – even to me.

Always uncomfortable with self-promotion, he knew that by choosing to dedicate himself for so long to a little-known rural backwater, he was forgoing the kind of attention he might have achieved if he had diversified, or taken on more glamorous or controversial subjects: a place internationally well known like the Lake District, for instance; or an eye-catching 'issue' such as inner-city problems. He turned down some outside commissions because he never felt his work in Devon was done. He was always nagged by the feeling that there were scenes still missing from his tapestry; and, actually, he didn't really want to work away from home on his own. Perhaps because of his childhood, he always disliked partings, however short.

His pursuit of beauty, which was so important to him, was unfashionable, too. Painterly effects that he strived hard to capture on film meant little in the contemporary world of photography where being arresting, challenging, *different*, seemed to matter so much more. He also felt an alien in the world of what he called 'artbollocks' (a *Private Eye* term, I think). He despised jargon, and impenetrable 'artists' statements' full of pretentious claims and concepts. He used to groan at the self-consciousness of that kind of thing. His approach was not an intellectual one. He took what he saw spontaneously, because it interested, moved or amused him – or because it made a composition he enjoyed. And he wanted his pictures to speak for themselves without complex explanation, or the intrusion of his personal views.

The archive soon came to dominate our lives: it occupied our living space, dictated our movements, and often took James away when other husbands would have been at home. On Christmas Day, for instance, he was quite likely to disappear to take someone else's celebrations. He disliked Christmas anyway – his hackles rose at any jollity which seemed to him false or 'compulsory'. It was a little sad for me; we had had very traditional English festivals at home because my father loved them; but I understood James's attitude. Like Tirzah, I accepted that his work came first for him, just as it had for both our fathers. I'd learned in childhood to respect the needs of the artist at the head of the family. In any case, it was a constant pleasure to see the portrait of my homeland growing year by year.

As a dad, James was benign, if semi-detached. He wanted children, and enjoyed them in a casual way, but he left their upbringing to me. He didn't do discipline, and never volunteered for the hands-on care – though he could

manage it if he had to. On the rare occasions when I needed to be away, he coped pretty well, though he regularly overlooked the instructions and lists that I supplied. The nourishing meals I left ready to save him trouble were often still in the fridge when I got home because, 'Oh, I didn't see them,' or because going out for fish and chips and Mars bars had been more appealing. The children made no complaint. Nor did he particularly care about feeding their minds, to me the most rewarding part of child-rearing. But we went on family outings, and cheap caravan holidays by the sea when we could afford them. He photographed us all a good deal, but chiefly in order to use up a strip of film so that he could get on with processing the endless trial shots he took to test lenses, light settings or materials; although if there were lovely family pictures among them, as there often were, he regretted it because I would pester him for lots of annoyingly small prints for Christmas cards.

Archie Parkhouse and Jo Curzon serving their Christmas dinner,
Horseshoe Cottage, Dolton, 1982
James Ravilious/Beaford Archive

On the plus side, because of our cramped quarters, Ben and Ella saw far more of him and his work than children of a nine-to-five worker would have done. They were dripped on by his prints from an early age as they played on the sitting room floor. They heard work talk going on all the time, and mingled with his official visitors. They were often nearby when he was taking photos; or else waiting with me by the car somewhere because he had spotted a likely subject, parked abruptly, grabbed the camera bag and disappeared, leaving us with no idea when we would see him again. We did a lot of nature study in hedges while we waited for him, and I learnt never to travel without supplies. But if his working hours and methods were unconventional, he set the children a fine example of dedication to his job.

Ben, Robin, Ella, James and Rumpus the cat, Addisford, 1985,
taken with a long cable release
James Ravilious

As they grew older, he did much patient chauffeuring, to school, ortho-
dontist, clubs and friends, using the trips to look for photo opportunities. He
started Ben off on the Airfix models that he had loved as a boy; and shared his
technical enthusiasms with him. Ben got a computer long before I thought it
necessary, or affordable; James foresaw its importance. But also he was longing
to play with it himself.

I used to envy his single-mindedness. Being a Jill of several trades myself
but mistress of none, and having always to multi-task as most wives and
mothers do, I longed for his ability to shut out everything except the work in
hand. It was impressive to see the pains he would take when he had an enthusiasm on the boil. But it could be a disadvantage. The obsessively long hours
he worked in the darkroom did him no good; and his absent-mindedness
could make life difficult. He was seldom in time for meals. He said himself,
'There ought to be a Society for the Protection of Photographers' Wives.' One
could never wholly rely on him to remember anything: appointments, errands,
shopping – or even a five-year-old, forlornly kicking gravel at the school
gate. More than one important visitor who came a long way to see his work
was met at the door with a completely blank look from James while, in the
background, I was frantically scuffling away the toys, nappies and plates of
baked beans, among which the archive had to live in those days. He also lost
things with monotonous regularity: vital papers, cheque books, spectacles,
wallets, hats – too many hats to count, though some of those I didn't much
regret.

Sometimes his forgetfulness brought him close to catastrophe. In 1981
when he and Tony Foster were planning the Cévennes trip they made a date
to travel up to London together, by coach to save money, for an interview at
the French Embassy about sponsorship for the trip. At the same time James
was to take a precious portfolio containing his share of his father Eric's
unframed work to the Fine Arts Society with a view to raising funds by selling

something from it. This was our only 'back up', our last resort when cash was urgently needed for photo equipment, thatching, car repairs or some other frightening bill. James met Tony at Exeter bus station early in the morning and they set off together. About fifteen miles up the motorway somewhere near Tiverton, an appalling realisation dawned. The portfolio had not come too.

He had put it down on – of all things – a rubbish bin. James being James, he tackled the coach driver with desperate pleas and succeeded in persuading him to pause, quite illegally, on the hard shoulder. Promising to meet Tony at the Embassy, James leapt off the coach, hared up the embankment and over fences *and* the main railway line, and slogged through fields to an approach road where he could hitch his way back to Exeter. An hour or two later, when he returned to the bus station, the rubbish bin had been emptied, and the portfolio was gone. But a cleaner was sweeping nearby. Yes, he had found the portfolio but he hadn't thought it looked like rubbish so he had handed it in. I strongly suspect that James, giddy with relief, will have given him a handsome tip before hurrying across Exeter to catch an expensive train. He missed the Embassy appointment, of course.

By the time I knew him, James was not a book reader. He read newspapers, *Private Eye* and art or photography magazines and manuals avidly, but not books . . . with two important exceptions. He loved Flaubert's *Madame Bovary*. A battered copy went with him on trips and journeys, and even into hospital. I used to think it extraordinary that he of all people should like such a cold-hearted story; but later I realised that he probably skipped most of the human interaction. Flaubert once wrote: 'Anything is interesting if you look at it long enough,' and it was his minutely detailed, almost photographic, descriptions of everyday rural life in nineteenth-century France that fascinated James. Apparently the American photographer, Walker Evans, whom James admired, had a passion for Flaubert for the same reason.

The other favourite companion was a collection of poems by Edward Thomas. In general, though James responded readily to the visually poetic, he shied away from spoken or written poetry – it seemed to make him uncomfortable. But Thomas's quiet, unadorned style, with its plain but vivid evocations of countryside, spoke to him powerfully.

He often *bought* books, however. Art books were a weakness of his – though he could seldom afford new publications. Whenever we visited towns and cities he would home in on second-hand bookshops and hunt through the arts section greedily. He didn't even mind if the editions were in a foreign language, or so old that the illustrations were in black-and-white. He still got a lot from them, for these were books to look at, not to read: sources to pore over again and again, drinking in composition and tone and draftsmanship.

When it came to writing, James was in trouble. Perhaps it was those obligatory Sunday letters home from school, or the dreary chore of essays, that had given him a mental block. Writing a business letter was for him an ordeal. At the end of a morning's struggle I would find him surrounded by screwed-up pages – usually of expensive headed notepaper – each bearing a sentence or two in his stylish italic hand, furiously scribbled out. If it was a report or article about his work it was even harder. At the end of angry and frustrated hours, as some urgent deadline loomed, he would bring the letter or article to me in despair, and I would take over. Some time later – usually after midnight – I would hand him my draft, he would skim through it far too rapidly to take it in, say, 'Brilliant, absolutely brilliant!' and put the whole thing right out of his head with relief. Until he started to use a computer in the 1990s, which loosened up his writing, I think there were few important letters, and nothing in print, which didn't go through this process. I even had to write his acknowledgement of me in one of his prefaces. Luckily, because he talked about his work so much, I usually knew ahead what he wanted to say.

Like many creative people, he had episodes of depression when he felt his spark had gone; there had been too long a gap since the last good photo. He would quote other photographers who had 'burnt out', as he called it. Often such patches were triggered by what he saw as the indifference of the Beaford administration.

He had the sort of high-strung temperament that can affect physical health; and after what he had been through in the past it was hardly surprising that he should have a touch of hypochondria. He had watched from a distance the stages of his mother's decline through a significant part of his childhood, and had endured cancer himself. From then on all symptoms had a threatening aspect; and he ailed quite frequently. In the time I knew him he had pleurisy, mumps, two hernias, repetitive strain injury, Bell's palsy, a recurring infection in his lower jaw, a mysteriously swollen knee and shingles. And every time he became stressed, he had a burning pain in the stomach which, after tests for duodenal ulcer and other horrors, was finally labelled 'nervous gastritis'. No cure was offered, but treatment from an acupuncturist friend had a soothing effect. The pain subsided when he calmed down.

By the late 1970s, after so many hours in the darkroom, he was also beginning to get an allergic reaction to some of the chemicals in fixative. They are now known to be irritant, and a possible carcinogen. An hour's printing would leave his whole respiratory tract sore, and give him flu-like symptoms of lethargy and depression, which would take several days to wear off. He battled on for years, exploring one method after another to avoid the fumes: trying to operate with clumsy rubber gloves and uncomfortable masks, constructing Heath Robinson air-filtering devices over the workbench, and installing an industrial-sized extractor fan. But fixative is insidious. It impregnated his clothes, and I could even smell it on his breath after a printing session. It may or may not have contributed to the cancer's return (we heard of several other darkroom workers who suffered from lymphoma.) Eventually, in the last few years, he was obliged to employ assistants to do most of the printing under his direction.

Whatever the problem, the current symptoms would fill his mind until he nerved himself to go to the doctor. But once a diagnosis was made he was always relieved, even if the symptoms persisted. At least it wasn't cancer again . . . yet. Deep down, he knew he was living on borrowed time.

18 . INSPIRATION

MOST CREATIVE PEOPLE ARE MOTIVATED by other artists to some extent. Either they try to emulate them out of admiration, or they want to see if they themselves can do better. James's artistic journey was inspired by some very diverse talents.

Unfortunately his parents weren't there to get him started, though they gave him his artistic genes. But I'm not sure his photography was *influenced* by them, though he was certainly proud of his father's work, and cared a great deal about the standards of presentation when exhibitions and books began to happen. However, father and son clearly enjoyed many of the same things: English light, abstract pattern, muted colouring, old-fashioned shops, old machinery and quirky corners of junk half-buried in nettles. They structured their images in similar ways. Both of them looked intensely at the ordinary, and made it extraordinary by their enjoyment of it. I imagine it was from Tirzah that he got his interest in people. And I like to think that his warm, gentle nature came from his Devon grandparent, Eric's mother Emma.

Peggy Angus was the first important creative influence in his adult life (as she was for many other people), for it was she who made him realise that he was an artist. His feelings towards her were gratitude – for he owed her a lot – mixed with occasional exasperation. Peggy demanded an enthusiastic response to all her notions and projects, and hammered home her views on any subject, which could be a little wearing at times. She always had firm ideas on what other people should be doing with their lives. But she was warm-hearted and full of inspiring life and energy, and he was very fond of her. She was proud of having rescued him from accountancy, though she disapproved

Downland in Winter, 1934 (watercolour)
Eric Ravilious/Towner Art Gallery, Eastbourne

when he later defected from paintings to photographs as she didn't consider photography a real art. 'Anyone can take photos,' she would say, dismissively. She came round slowly as his output increased, far enough to attend one of his London private views, and to pin a print of his peeing cow on her lavatory door. But she valued his early drawing of the sitting room at Furlongs, which he had given her, far more than any photo; and left it back to us in her will – as a testament to what might have been.

With *my* relations, James sometimes did the inspiring. His relationship with my father was one of guarded affection, for they were very different

The Hansom Cab and the Pigeons, 1935 (wood engraving)
Eric Ravilious

people. They appreciated each other's skills – both of them working in black-and-white, using light as their medium – and they shared a love of Wessex landscape and of Samuel Palmer. My father (and my brother Simon) used photographs by James as reference or inspiration for glass engravings. But James was ill at ease with the poetic side of my father's life view; while my father became bored with 'all those old farmers in their muddy boots'. He wanted to collaborate on a book to promote and celebrate James's most poetic pictures, for which he would write an accompanying text on his own ideas about light and landscape. But James was nervous of it. My father saw the real world in metaphysical terms; James relished the everyday for what it was. He never took up the offer.

Once, however, when we were staying at Halsdon Mill in the early days,

Test shot of moonlight and stream,
Halsdon Mill, Dolton, c. 1971
James Ravilious

James went out into the garden at night to take test shots in extreme low-light conditions. Among them was a mysterious photo of moonlight through the trees over the stream that looked exactly like a goblet engraved by my father. It was not in itself a great photo, but I sent him a print for his birthday, and he replied: 'What point for me in scratching away at glasses if Jas can do it all – in a twinkling – and much better, with his camera? It's a magical photograph, really quite outstanding, more magical because the stem of the goblet seems to be there, in the reflecting stream. Mummy would have been enchanted by it.'

James was introduced to the kind of photography he wanted to do by Cartier-Bresson's work. As he told an *Observer* journalist: 'One thing [Cartier-Bresson] taught me is that there is such a thing as The Moment. It is myste-

The Touch of Day (Halsdon Mill through trees), 1963
(engraved goblet)
Laurence Whistler

rious, but if you look at several shots of one scene, there is one that has it – as if there were a little poem in there – but only for a second.'

It was a sadness to him that he never talked to another of his heroes, Edwin Smith, about photography. Edwin had died of cancer in 1971. It was not until James became a professional photographer a year or so later that he began to look at Edwin's books, and realised how good he had been, and what a superb record of the landscape and buildings of Britain, the grand and the lowly, he had left to posterity. Edwin had an eye for humble objects: day-to-day bits and pieces, the unconsidered but revealing stuff that people accumulate. For James, too, the ordinary was always fascinating, and Edwin's pictures inspired him to make his own tributes to the eloquence of everyday things.

The support of Olive Cook, Edwin's wife, meant a lot to him. Though not a photographer herself, she was a discerning critic. A lovely person, very intelligent, warmly affectionate and enthusiastic, she had passionate views about life and art. I always felt she spoke in italics. She had had a very soft spot for *'Darling James!'* ever since their first meeting in 1946. I think he was the son she would have liked to have. She was delighted when he turned to photography. Much later, she wrote to me: 'I loved James from the time I first knew him as a very little boy. He already had enormous charm and a delightful sense of humour. I treasure every memory of our friendship.'

After his death she wrote an article, 'A Triumph of Evocation', about James's Beaford Archive work for *Matrix*, the journal of the typography world. She concluded with the words: 'I know of no other presentation of a particular place and people which is as broad and as captivating as James Ravilious's photographs of North Devon. They are the fruit of a quite exceptional acuity and patience of witness and of a quite unusual humility and warmth of spirit. This great body of work establishes its author as a master of the art of photography while at the same time it makes an unparalleled pictorial contribution to social history.'[7]

Family heirlooms, Deckport, Hatherleigh, 1977
James Ravilious/Beaford Archive

Though documentary photography was becoming popular in Britain at the time, James was not part of the contemporary scene. He took an interest, certainly, but he never pushed himself into it. He was quite critical of a lot of photographers, finding their work clever, but too detached or exploitative for his taste. Also, he had not done the training that most of them had, and I think that, coupled with his individualist approach, made him feel something of an outsider. However, another Devon photographer, Chris Chapman, was a long-term ally. Chris had contacted James in the 1970s because he was making his own black-and-white record of life on Dartmoor twenty miles away. They shared a love of Devon and its communities, and became great friends, going on photography walks together, and spending hours on the phone discussing darkroom problems and exchanging useful information, in the amiable non-competitive way that seems to be common in their profession. Both were always searching for the best film, the best paper, and the best chemicals for their purposes. Chris, being freelance rather than salaried, had a professional attitude to such things as finding commissions and selling prints. James was always acutely uncomfortable about promoting his work, or deciding what to charge for it. So Chris's advice could be very useful to him – if he took it.

Much of James's inspiration came not from photography at all, but from art. He looked at the real world with a reference library of European art at the back of his mind. Mediaeval art fascinated him. Illuminated manuscripts were an early interest. I had a facsimile edition of the book of hours, *Les Belles Heures*, created in around 1410 for Jean, Duc de Berry (possibly by the Flemish Limbourg brothers), which inspired him. He bought another of the allegorical courtly romance called *Le Livre du Cueur d'Amours Espris*, written, and possibly also illustrated, by René, Duc d'Anjou in 1457. The illustrations to this include wonderful effects of light: a dimly lit bedroom, sunrise, sunset and extraordinary night scenes by starlight. Later, James discovered Jean Fouquet (1420–81), French portrait painter and illuminator. Though many of these

works focus on great events in the Bible, or classical literature and history, what James particularly relished in them was the incidental detail, the views of everyday country life in the fifteenth century, in which those events are set.

He was also keen on mediaeval carving, whether it was miniaturised in ivory on reliquaries, on a larger scale in the oak of church benches, screens and roof bosses, or monumental in the stone of Gothic statuary. It was their energy, I think, which chimed for him with the life and landscape of North Devon. There is something about our countryside, its intimate scale, its unkemptness, which recalls the robust naivety of mediaeval art. It was a quality that James, who sometimes used odd words, called 'nuttiness', by which he meant the

Desire meets Modest Plea at Sunrise near Lord Amour's Encampment.
From *Le Livre du Cueur d'Amours Espris* by René, Duc d'Anjou, 1457,
Austrian National Library, Vienna

character of a woodcut: a chunky, rough-hewn vitality. His image of an oak tree at Marsland captures it well.

He loved the early Italian painters particularly for the arrangement of their figures. This can be seen in one of his images, *Spraying the Shorn Lamb, Addisford*. Even in this frankly basic task (the disinfecting of any cuts made by the shears which might attract blow-fly maggots), he saw and enjoyed the archetypal poses people adopt when intent on something. I'm not sure if it was conscious, but I know that he was responding to the scene just as he would have done to a grouping of shepherds in a Renaissance nativity scene, and composing his image accordingly.

He felt a special affinity with the rural chroniclers who came before him, from those mediaeval illuminators onwards. He was in a sense part of a

Oak tree (after Mondrian), Marsland, Devon, 1997
James Ravilious

long chain of artists who recorded the everyday. Some of the scenes he photographed were not all that different from those of the fifteenth century, for example, apart from the costumes; and that link was important to him. He felt a particular connection to the great wood-engraver, Thomas Bewick, whose miniature vignettes celebrate the countryside of Northumberland at the end of the eighteenth century. Bewick worked in much the same way as James, recording the life of the country he loved and lived in: real people and real scenes that he saw as he walked to and fro between his childhood home, Cherryburn, overlooking the River Tyne, and his printing workshop eleven miles downstream in Newcastle. Even on the tiny 'canvas' of his little boxwood blocks, Bewick portrayed weather and landscape, work and play, hardship, cruelty, humour and pathos, with the honesty which James so much admired.[8]

Spraying the shorn lamb, Addisford, Dolton, 1985
James Ravilious/Beaford Archive

The Skylark, 1850 (etching) by Samuel Palmer
Private collection

Artists who were experts in conveying light were always favourites. James had an edition of Claude Lorrain's *Liber Veritatis*, the 'catalogue' he made in swift pen-and-wash sketches to record his paintings before he parted with them. To James (and to many painters) it was a masterclass on composition and luminosity in landscape work.

Then there was Samuel Palmer, who had been my favourite painter since childhood. James knew that he had meant a lot to Eric, but he hadn't looked at his work in detail. He soon came to see a similarity to our area in Palmer's landscape paintings. Though we didn't know it then, Palmer wrote of his 'intense love' for North Devon after a painting trip he made there in 1835. With its bosomy hills, its thatched buildings half-buried in wooded combes, and its cornfields full of stooks, our countryside can still be a living

Apple tree, early morning,
West Park, Iddesleigh, c. 1985
James Ravilious

193

embodiment of Palmer's visionary country. Even its colouring is reminiscent of his palette sometimes, especially in spring when the new leaf on the oak woods burns with his wonderful ochreous glow.

James was far too much of a realist to be a visionary in Palmer's sense, but he enormously admired Palmer's control of light. It was the later work, the etchings, which impressed him most of all. He said in an interview: 'I am really trying to do a Samuel Palmer with what I see.' Palmer wrote that his goal was 'the glimmering through of the paper even in the shadows so that almost everything either sparkles or suggests sparkle.'[9] The superb tonal range Palmer achieved in his moonlit skies, his evening sunbeams through trees, and his summer dawns inspired James in his struggle to get his equipment to give him the light effects he wanted.

Snow scene, children in donkey panniers, from
A General History of Quadrupeds, 1790,
(wood engraving) by Thomas Bewick

19 . TECHNICAL PROGRESS

JAMES HAD CHOSEN the rangefinder Leica camera because Cartier-Bresson used one, and because it had long been popular for documentary work as it was quiet, unobtrusive and relatively simple to use. He taught himself to use it as he went along by reading manuals and articles, and by trial and error. To begin with he fitted his Leica M3 body with modern Leitz lenses such as the 35mm and 50mm Summicrons. Their quality made his early negatives 'contrasty' – that is, distinctly black or white, with few subtleties of tone in between, not unlike woodcuts at times. He had to work hard to produce any nuance in skies when he printed from them. Also, detail in interiors was difficult to achieve using only available light, as he chose to do. When he came to evaluate them later on, he would judge these first images harshly, labelling many of them 'very contrasty', or 'difficult to print'. But once he had mastered the camera settings, the kit as a whole was ideal for swift manipulation in the heat of the moment, and produced images that were quite adequate for the historical record he was making. The artist in him would come to want more later on.

Like Cartier-Bresson, he had elected to work with black-and-white film rather than colour. A practical reason for this was that it lasted longer than the colour film available at the time, and was therefore better for an archive. But it was also an aesthetic choice. He called it 'more profound', feeling that the spirit of an image was more accessible, and more affecting, without the distractions of colour. To him it was actually more *real*. He may have been influenced in this by the old black-and-white films that he loved and was moved by: *Bicycle Thieves* and *Closely Observed Trains,* for instance, and *Pather Panchali* by the great Indian film director Satyajit Ray.

He did do work in colour from time to time – at his own expense. For obviously colourful subjects such as carnivals, flower shows and certain landscapes, he usually carried Kodachrome 25 colour transparency film in a second camera as well as his normal outfit. But the slides it made were taken more for their possible commercial value in reproduction than their artistic merit. They were not included in the archive, and he never did much with them.

Another major objection to colour work was that he had too little control over it. The hues were governed largely by the film itself, and by the processes of the commercial firms who printed it. Their colours were unnatural, far too garish for his taste – especially the greens, which were usually so aggressively bright and harsh that he felt they completely unbalanced a composition, a serious problem for someone working in a countryside where the fields are cushions of emerald velvet for a large part of the year. James shared the view of a number of the Old Masters that strong green was a 'difficult' colour to incorporate harmoniously in a painting, and that therefore it was best avoided as much as possible. Like the eighteenth-century watercolourists, and Eric who had been inspired by them, he favoured muted colours in landscape work. I was surprised sometimes to hear him go into raptures over the colours of, say, a clouded winter landscape just before dusk, when all that I could see was pale olive, fawn and shades of grey just tinted with a faint wash of pink. I

used to wonder if his colour vision was more subtle than mine.

At one point, he invested in the equipment to do his own colour printing (processes with even more unhealthy chemicals than monochrome), hoping to get more realistic colours, but it was extremely taxing work, and seldom pleased him, so he abandoned it quite soon.

He was not entirely satisfied with his black-and-white photos, either. Some years into the Beaford Archive project, perhaps as a result of seeing his work as a body in *The Heart of the Country*, he became unhappy with his modern lenses, finding their sharp black/white contrast inadequate both for suggesting form, and for recording the sparkle and softness that was so typical of North Devon's rain-washed climate. He began to take a more technical interest in equipment and processes, and consulted others in his field. The

Stooks and rainbow, Westacott, Riddlecombe, c. 1985
James Ravilious

photographer's guru, Brian Allen, was very helpful to him. In the early 1980s, at Brian's suggestion, he began to experiment with different lenses. His notes record several false starts: 'Contrasty pic, using new lens, horridly contrasty,' or 'New Leica lens Much too contrasty. Sold it!' But then in August 1981, on the back of his contact sheet of the young bulls eating thistles, comes a note 'Testing 73mm Hektor lens Uncoated!' He had begun to trawl through small advertisements and second-hand camera shops for pre-war lenses which didn't have the fluoride coating of their modern counterparts so that their effect was softer. Some were 'too fuzzy', but others, such as the Hektors and Elmars made by Leitz in the 1920s and '30s, pleased him, though he sometimes had to improvise arrangements of his own in order to attach them to the M3 camera body by sacrilegiously filing bits off, or bolting them on. (James rose to any small engineering challenge, confident that he could improve on a bit of equipment by using whatever methods and materials came to hand, however unorthodox. If he couldn't buy the part he needed, he dismantled something, misapplied something, or cut up my saucepans and Tupperware.)

James's Leica camera, as modified
George Tucker

In order to make best use of these old lenses he also created an eccentric adaptation for his lens hoods using his old friend, electrician's tape: he masked off the edges of the hoods to reduce their frames to fit the exact image areas of the lenses. This allowed him to shoot almost into the sun, as he loved to do, without losing too much detail in dark areas, and without getting too much flare on his negatives.

Brian Allen also introduced him to the American photographer Ansel Adams's books on photography and, in particular, to Adams's 'Zone' compensation technique, a system of slightly over-exposing a film, and then slightly under-developing it, in order to produce a greater tonal range in the resulting print. James was excited by the graphic qualities this could give him: subtle detail in shadows, and a sense of depth, of three-dimensional form, in his

Alf Pugsley returning a lamb to its mother,
Langham, Dolton, 1982
James Ravilious/Beaford Archive

photographs – the thing that he had cared about so much in a drawing. Now he could work towards the 'silver watercolour' quality he wanted. It was an important breakthrough.

Hunting in the second-hand market, he also came across a Leitz's auxiliary viewfinder, the VIOOH (known as the 'Vee-oo') which could be slotted on to the top of a camera for a clearer view of a scene as a complete framed entity than a built-in viewfinder could give – the equivalent of standing back from the easel for an artist, which made composing both easier and much more precise, even at speed.

Another discovery was lens filters. When he was reviewing his work in the 1990s, James returned to some unsatisfactory negatives he had taken in 1982 and marked his record: 'Trying to get clouds, learnt about filters later!!!!'

Storm cloud and geese, Indiwell, Swimbridge, 1985
James Ravilious/Beaford Archive

Some time after that date he tried out a light yellow '0' filter on his lenses, and used it for most of his work thereafter. Clouds could now become major actors in a photograph.

At around the same time, James decided to explore plate cameras. So he built himself one from scratch: a monster like some of the nineteenth-century cameras, a 10" × 13" × 7" box of wood and aluminium with brass and steel drawer handles to carry it by, which took individual 8½" × 6½" plate negatives in a metal frame, and which required long exposures. It weighed well over seven pounds. Like the early photographers, he had to compose his pictures in it upside down (though that was not a hardship to James, who had always taught that a drawing should be assessed that way). He needed a large wooden tripod, and a black light-proof cloth over his head, to operate it. But the silvery grainless print quality it produced, and the depth of field, were, for a time, worth the effort of lugging the whole outfit about. One of his best landscapes, *View Towards Iddesleigh and Dartmoor*, was taken with this giant. He had photographed that particular scene over and over again, at different seasons and different times of day, and in several different formats, but this large-format early-morning version pleased him most. I'm sure that Claude Lorrain was at the back of his mind when he took it. Claude had had sun-baked Italian rocks and ruins and the distant Appenines to work with; James was happy with the shaggy wooded reaches of mid-Devon and Dartmoor's rippling profile beyond.

The home-made camera proved a bit too cumbersome for everyday use but James also had another, much smaller, plate camera which he now began to explore. It was one of Edwin Smith's main cameras – an old bellows model manufactured in the 1920s called an Ica. Olive had been told that 'no one today would dream of using such equipment'. She gave it to James, saying, 'I know Edwin would wish it and I feel you are an artist and could use the instrument in his vein.' The Ica took individual slides of film, in 5" × 7" or

View towards Iddesleigh and Dartmoor, c. 1985
(taken on the large plate camera)
James Ravilious

6cm × 9cm formats, which had to be slotted in and out for each exposure so James could use it only for fairly static subjects such as landscapes, still lifes and portraits. He customised it in his usual fashion to take his choice of lenses and a VIOOH viewfinder, and used it for much of his later private work. The whole system imposed a different kind of discipline to that of the nimble Leica: more planned, more selective, and more consciously artistic. He loved to use it for Edwin's sake, and took landscapes and buildings (including one in the garden at Halsdon Mill, which would have appealed to Edwin particularly, I think), as well as plant studies and a series on the mediaeval carving in our local churches, which he hoped to make into a book one day.

The combination of technique, old-fashioned equipment and eccentric adaptations allowed James to approach a photograph more as a graphic artist would. All three contributed to the quality he is most admired for: what John Lane called his 'lyrical naturalism'. But although he put a lot of thought and a lot of careful trials into his various technical developments, I don't think they ever took over. He never aimed to make prints that were artworks in their own

Edwin Smith's Ica camera, modified by James
George Tucker

right. For him, the technical stuff was always a means to an end: capturing the *real* light of common day.

I have summarised James's photographic practice very briefly here; it was more complex and varied than I'm qualified to describe. Peter Hamilton's introduction to his book *An English Eye – The Photographs of James Ravilious* gives a much more knowledgeable and detailed account.

Ella in the garden of Halsdon Mill, Dolton, 1984
(taken on the Ica)
James Ravilious

20 . CHANGE

ENCOURAGED BY MY SMALL PART in *All Around The Year* I had begun to draw again, under James's critical eye. The children and I used to take our daily walks past Archie's dilapidated henhouse at the crossroads between his cottage and ours. Here a motley flock of hens led a free-range existence, foraging in the woods and ditches, and roosting in an elder tree. Since we usually came bearing gifts the whole scruffy band would pour like windblown leaves down the road to meet us, and snatch the crusts from the children's hands. We got to know them well, and I took to drawing them, and studying their individual personalities. This led to my first picture book for young children, *The Runaway Chick*. A few years later another, *Two In A Pocket,* was inspired by the dormouse which arrived one spring in a bundle of thatching straw for our roof, still so deep asleep that I was able to hold it in one hand while I drew it with the other, recording its slow awakening. James was encouraging. He approved my drawings of natural life, though he deplored the indecisive way I sometimes worked: beginning on a detail instead of planning the whole design properly first. He was right, of course; it often cost me dear to pull it all together at the end. One or two other writing and illustration jobs followed, and it was good to be doing something creative again, for myself, though finding space and time to do it was always difficult in those days.

Our tiny cottage had never been the tranquil white cell I yearned for; we were too swamped with possessions, and too untidy. By the middle of the 1980s it was bursting at the seams. Ben and Ella were getting too old to share their narrow slice of bedroom, and needed space to do their own thing. It really wasn't possible for so much of our work, hobbies and homework to happen in one room. We could not afford to extend the cottage again; the children's friends were all too far away; and being nearest neighbour to my stepmother for the past nine years had at intervals been extremely difficult. In 1986 we took the painful decision to sell and move closer to civilisation. Eventually we found an early Victorian terrace house going for several thousand pounds less than the value of Addisford. It was in Chulmleigh, a small town half an hour east of Dolton.

Leaving Addisford next year at the height of an unfairly beautiful spring was a heartbreaking wrench for me, despite all the cogent reasons for going. It felt like my childhood exile from Halsdon all over again; and also a kind of betrayal to sell my grandfather's gift, and to cut the ties with my deepest roots, though we held on to our little bit of wood as a token foothold. Admittedly, the countryside round Chulmleigh was just as beautiful and unspoilt as the Dolton area. But it didn't 'belong' to us in the way that Halsdon had always seemed to do. (Though, by that time, my uncle Patrick Furse had sold the big house and Ashwell Farm to a private buyer, and part-sold, part-gifted the woods and river valley to the Devon Wildlife Trust.) Also, the new country was a walk away. The house was on a street, and had no views at all. We would lose the sense we had had at Addisford of nature coming in at the door.

But for James it seemed like an inviting new beginning. He drove the eight miles between the two houses to and fro for weeks transferring our portable possessions, and doing energetic DIY ahead of the main move. He enjoyed planning and doing up a new home, and was excited by the prospect of fresh territory to record. Now he would have a different landscape to explore in depth, and the everyday life of a pleasant, rather French, little town on his doorstep providing subjects he felt he hadn't covered well enough as yet.

There were other benefits too. For Ben and Ella the move meant schools they could walk to and friends nearby, as well as a large room each where they could have space and privacy, two things which I had longed for as a teenager. For us there was the convenience of shops, doctor and dentist a few yards from the door.

Now at last we had smooth vertical walls we could hang pictures on, and it was possible to find homes for more books and a few attractive possessions, and to expand James's hi-fi system. In the next months he made art-book-sized bookshelves and added extra cupboards in the kitchen; and in the small high-walled garden at the back he converted an old shed into a greenhouse for me. He also transformed the brutal slab-framed fireplace in the sitting room with a simple Victorian wooden fire-surround which we bought from an architectural salvage depot. The following year we had the roof space of the house converted into three attic workrooms: a darkroom, an exhibition and negative storage room, and a workshop for James.

But we had not really been able to leave my family problems or his work issues behind us; and in addition I was advised to have a hysterectomy that autumn. Soon my elderly father, far away in Oxfordshire, began to need my support. The years that followed were not as bright as we had hoped. James became depressed again about his relationship with Beaford, feeling that the archive would never be valued there until long after his death. It was a grey time for both of us.

In the following year he was temporarily rescued from low spirits by a part-time commission from the pioneering arts and environment charity

Common Ground. Its founders Sue Clifford and Angela King admired his work, and in 1988 invited him to record orchards in the south-west for an exhibition to spearhead their campaign to rescue old orchards from extinction and to revive the English apple in all its wonderful variety. It was part of their wider purpose which was to promote 'local distinctiveness', to celebrate, by means of artists' work, communal events, and books, the objects, sights and customs which are unique to individual areas of Britain.

This was exactly the kind of thing James loved to do, but he was so depressed at the time that he was all for turning it down. He had convinced himself that he was no longer capable of doing it. However, I managed to persuade him into a reconnaissance trip to Somerset before he made up his

Orchard at Whimple, 1989
James Ravilious

mind, and he was won over. The delightful old orchard men we encountered, and the charm of the orchards we found, both ancient and modern, seduced him. It was autumn when he made his first forays, so we wandered in gothic aisles of veteran trees weighed down by glowing fruit: pale green, golden or sunset-streaked. We breathed in the cidrous scent of windfalls, and scrambled about among trees that had long since tilted over to lie on their elbows in the nettles still fruiting away regardless. On trips in Somerset, Devon and further afield to west Dorset and Cornwall, we learnt the historic local names for the

Pear orchard in blossom,
Combe Florey, Somerset, 1989
James Ravilious

JAMES RAVILIOUS: A LIFE

hundreds of different varieties: Slack Ma Girdle, Hoary Morning, Pig's Nose, Stripey Jack, and their many different qualities which had long been cherished locally for eating, cooking or cider-making. The following spring James returned to capture the blossom, when the trees were snowed under and even more beautiful.

It was his most rewarding short commission. The pictures became a travelling exhibition, and later featured in a couple of books, while the whole Save Our Orchards campaign, with the inauguration of Apple Day, has been responsible for a change in attitudes to orchards in England. James was happy to be a part of this. A set of the best photos was later bought for the Royal Devon and Exeter Hospital, to hang in a corridor there, lifting the spirits of patients and their visitors. Common Ground was an ideal commissioner, considerate, helpful and appreciative throughout the process, creating the perfect atmosphere for an artist to flourish in.

Sometimes, when stress about the situation with Beaford became too much, James would talk about pulling up sticks altogether and moving right away from North Devon, to France if possible, abandoning the archive to its fate. I'm not sure if he would really have gone through with it, but in any case it seemed wrong to me, as well as impractical, and very hard on the children at that time. After a bad patch at the end of the 1980s when the pay was inadequate and a particular relationship extremely difficult, he came up with a temporary solution: he would ask for a year's sabbatical, unpaid, in order to try and find a way forward. This was agreed in August 1990. He was assured in writing that his job would be kept open for him.

But the sabbatical didn't really achieve its objective; and paid work was scarce, apart from a short photography course at Plymouth University which he led with Jem Southam, the Professor of Photography there. He also went on giving talks locally, to camera clubs and other groups, but these, though enjoyable, paid little more than his petrol. An exhibition of his work was shown at the Curwen Gallery in London, and Common Ground's *Orchards* exhibition, with many of his images in it, was circulating widely. He also got himself some tuition to improve his computer skills. But otherwise it was an unproductive year.

As always, when he was in low spirits, James would try to distract himself with other interests. One of the most preoccupying of these was music. He loved all sorts of music, from Kathryn Tickell on the Northumbrian pipes to Wanda Landovska playing Bach on the harpsichord to John Fahey on the folk guitar. He almost always had the radio on in the darkroom when at work, and he listened to any music, classical or popular, with close attention. He would develop sudden enthusiasms for a South African guitarist, or Chinese pipes, or classical pieces on the accordion. It seemed to me, brought up on more expressive Romantic styles, that the common denominator in his choices was *precision* playing, above all else.

He had tinkered with his hi-fi system periodically since the 1960s, updating his speakers from time to time, but now he set himself to build a valve amplifier – no mean electronic feat. Like his photographic outfit, it was old-fashioned, but he felt it could serve him better than modern equivalents. As before with photography, he scoured magazines and manuals, and consulted experts (chiefly his brother John, for whom building speakers was an obsession) and tested, tested, tested everything he made. Little packages from Maplin's plopped on our mat by every post while, in his attic eyrie, a colourful deep litter accumulated underfoot composed of bright snippets of wire, dollops of surplus solder, and handfuls of capacitors, those tiny colour-banded electronic components that look like fairy toffees. The smell of hot solder was added to the stink of chemicals upstairs. Again, he was never quite satisfied, listening intently, and forever tweaking to make tiny improvements to the sound quality which were beyond my ears to appreciate.

The other distraction was a return to painting after over twenty years.

One day in 1990 he announced that he was going to try small paintings in egg tempera like the mediaeval illuminators – something that had been on his mind right back in 1969 when he wrote to me from Furlongs that first summer. He sent off to artists' colourmen for powder pigments, and left half-used egg-yolks congealing in the fridge, as he embarked on little bright landscapes unlike anything he had done before. Suddenly, with mediaeval manuscripts as his inspiration, he allowed himself vivid colour, though of a softly glowing kind. Later he used a synthetic medium in place of the egg. Some of the earliest pictures were almost abstract, but he also painted from memory the kind of landscapes he was photographing. One or two are actually based directly on archive images he had taken. As usual, he was seldom entirely satisfied, so there were many abandoned attempts.

In the following August, when the sabbatical year was up, James went back for a meeting with the Beaford management. For once I went with him,

Landscape with old barn beside a wood, c. 1995 (tempera)
James Ravilious

for moral support. During a long discourse from the director on the centre's dire financial position, it gradually became clear that the archive project was ending, and there was no job for James to return to after all, though I had to ask outright to make sure as he was silent with shock. We left the meeting quietly. After seventeen years' inadequately paid work, some 75,000 negatives of North Devon bequeathed to posterity, plus exhibitions, publications and reviews taking the name of Beaford to a national audience, that was that. There was no apology; no compensation; no acknowledgement of his work; no farewell occasion or letter; just the feeling that the management was relieved that a line had been drawn at last.

To have one's life's work so casually brought to an end is bound to be painful for anyone. To James, it was a body blow. The archive was his purpose in life: it mattered far more to him than any other work. And there was also a sense of outrage that he had been made to feel that he was leaving under a cloud, an implied accusation that he hadn't earned even his meagre keep. A more self-assured man might have challenged all this, but James didn't have the necessary ego.

Could more funding have been found for him, had the will been there? Perhaps not. It is not proving much easier these days, despite his growing reputation. Was it reasonable to close down his work after so long? Beaford's management, or its funders, obviously thought so. Seventeen years was an unprecedented length of time for such a project, especially one that was not considered central to the organisation's work (which was by then far more involved in the performance arts than the visual). Would it actually have been better for James to move on? He would after all have had to leave one day. I don't know the answers to these questions, but I do sometimes wonder how different things might have been if we had moved to France after all; if he had been able to forget the whole painful situation and immerse himself in a new project, in a country that really values photography.

It was a peculiar relationship that he had with Beaford, governed by what are now out-of-date copyright laws. After the law changed in 1989, few photographers other than press ones would have had to agree, as James did in 1974, to having so little control over the future of their work. But then no one at that time could have foreseen that 'a few photographs' by an amateur photographer would grow into a vast document of artistic and historic value. A busy, cash-strapped office dedicated to providing entertainment in far-flung rural communities was not cut out to deal with such a collection.

In the event he could not move on completely. His agreement tied him to Beaford unavoidably for the rest of his life because any major plans he wanted to make for the future of his work had to be approved by the director and governors. One archiving task was funded through them on a freelance basis.

21 . AFTER BEAFORD

APART FROM THE PAIN of that situation, the loss of a regular income, however small, became a worry. But we sold one of Eric's paintings, and generous friends and relations sent unexpected cheques. There were various small photographic commissions, and a few print sales. James also continued with his slide presentations to local schools, camera clubs and WI groups, though they brought in tiny sums that bore no relation to the amount of work he put into creating high-quality slides and tailoring their selection to each particular audience.

He was now increasingly anxious about his legacy to North Devon. Would the fragile negatives be taken care of, and would the collection be accessible to the audience for which it had been made? The first anxiety was allayed when, with the enthusiastic support of Louise Rose, the first North Devon Archivist, he persuaded Beaford to sign an agreement for the seventy-seven files of negatives to be stored in the strongroom of the North Devon Record Office in Barnstaple. This offered safe keeping and controlled atmospheric conditions for them. It was tedious for him to have to drive nineteen miles each way to fetch and carry them for printing, but he felt they would be safest there. They were there until 2015 when they were moved down to the Devon Heritage Centre in Exeter.

To ensure that at least some of his best images would be preserved in exhibition-standard prints that were as he wanted them, he negotiated with North Devon District Council who eventually agreed to buy two hundred. The original number discussed was four hundred, but James's allergy to the chemicals prevented him from printing so they had to be made by his friend and colleague Bryony Harris under his supervision. She was paid by the council, so the order was halved. James received a fee of £500. This was at a time when he sold such prints privately at £75 each. Those prints are now stored and sometimes exhibited in the North Devon Museum in Barnstaple.

A third concern was to make a proper record of the information known only to him about the content of his photos because, so far, there was nothing more than the hasty notes of date, place and people that he had scribbled on the backs of the contact sheets at the time of printing them. An archive required a catalogue in a standard retrieval format. Luckily, Beaford agreed that a computer database was necessary, and they were able to obtain funding to pay him £4,000, in three instalments, to research and compile it. So, with some professional training, and a nationally compatible program approved by the South West Museum Service, he began the massive task. Laborious as it was, it was something he could work at when he didn't feel up to anything else, and it helped to keep his mind occupied. Also it involved using a computer, which he enjoyed, and which had a liberating effect on his writing. Even so, it was a daunting prospect to compose what turned out to be 8,371 entries with accuracy and consistency, filling in a form with contact sheet and negative numbers, subject groups, locality, personal names, activity, notes, date taken, photographer and more, for every single entry. (It was 8,371 entries rather than 75,000 because he clumped many of the least interesting shots of a topic together.) Quite a lot of the entries required research, or even going back to the site of the photo for verification or extra information. As he worked, he graded his images, labelling them Best, Good, Fair or Poor, and snipping out any negatives that were useless. The Best (401 of them) and the Good (1,300) met his artistic standards as photographs and compositions as well as factual records. The huge majority were either Fair or Poor in his eyes; he thought little of them as photos, but left them in because their content was, or might become, of historic interest.

James was not by nature either academic or plodding but he stuck with perseverance to the grind of it, despite poor health and low spirits, doing a little every day. It took him many months. He relieved the tedium from time to time by adding characteristic personal comments in the Additional Notes column such as 'Very very boring picture of a lovely landscape!', 'Why did I take so many utterly dreary photos??????' or 'Farmer in sunlit shed with cow smoking a pipe, no, the farmer not the cow, silly!' In the Activity column there might be 'ploughing', 'thatching', 'chatting', or even 'mooing', but for one group of empty landscapes there is just an exclamation mark, in six successive entries.

Aware that he was making a public document, he was sensitive to people's feelings. On a touching portrait of Bill Cooke of Riddlecombe, the local historian farmer he was fond of, he comments: 'A wonderful man!' But another picture of Bill looking very mournful is marked: 'Sad pic, do not use.' Similarly, a tender shot of a couple after their wedding is labelled: 'Sadly, they later separated. Use with great caution! Do not name.' It was not, of course, possible to avoid featuring some people who would die premature and tragic deaths. He could only hope that their relatives wouldn't be too distressed to come across his pictures of them in the public domain.

His vocabulary is not always as consistent as it needs to be, and his spelling causes one or two hiccups, but his database does its job and is indispensable. Scrolling through it is a moving experience for me. In the descriptive column you can see over seventeen years of life in North Devon passing by, with words like 'lambing', 'shearing', 'haymaking', 'fair', 'harvest festival', 'Christmas', coming up again and again, as if you were riding a time machine: the annual wheel of local life rolling on and on. The weather itself is a major player: storms that brought down trees and loosed dramatic floods; the drought of 1977 when pastures were pale as straw and our stream stopped running; the blizzards of 1978 when the lanes filled with ten-foot drifts and the village was cut off. It is poignant to think how much human life is encompassed in that list – both commonplace, and unique. Much of it would have slipped into oblivion in one or two generations but for James. Woven into it (and still giving me little jolts when I come across them) are pictures of us, our own personal story: extending our cottage; ante-natal classes before Ben's birth in 1974; his schooldays; Ella's babyhood in 1980 and so on, for James had included these as part of his work, part of the huge tapestry which he was constantly stitching.

22 . LIGHT AND SHADE

THE GREY PERIOD CONTINUED, and James's heart was now causing concern. He was sent to a cardiologist in Barnstaple. Then, in the spring of 1993, he began to feel unwell: always tired, and slightly shivery. He developed mysterious complaints: very itchy skin with no sign of inflammation, and soaking sweats at night. Confusingly, on top of the heart trouble, he was also suffering from the recurring darkroom sensitivity and a very painful knee, so that his symptoms were rather a blur. What with seemingly endless tests, X-rays for possible chest infection and visits to all the different specialists, it took almost two months before a completely new one, a haematologist, suddenly appeared at his hospital bedside after a test and gently announced that he had bad news for us. It was lymphoma again. But this time it was a slow-burning version, Non-Hodgkin's variety, which was not curable, but which might be controlled with drugs. Chemotherapy started three days later.

So began the long cat-and-mouse game: six years of blood tests and scans and treatments; of encouraging news, and bad; of feeling better, and feeling worse. To begin with there were five months of chemotherapy, which meant day-long trips to North Devon District Hospital in Barnstaple every two weeks. James found the whole process exhausting to the nerves as he hated injections, but he put on his usual front of cheerful talk with the delightful chemo unit nurses.

Friends and admirers wrote to me after his death about his 'brave battle with cancer'. James's bravery was not the stiff-lipped hero sort. It was the courage of a frightened man trying to keep his fear out of sight for other people's sake. Tirzah wrote in her autobiography, 'It seemed to me to be bad-mannered to worry other people with your private miseries.' I think James felt the same. He didn't want to embarrass people. He talked to friends and relations freely about his treatment, and how it was going – ringing round to keep them up to date after any medical milestone – but he always managed to make it sound as if it were undramatic and commonplace. Only to me did he show the sickening dread he felt each time another exhausting test or hospital visit loomed; and the ordeal it was for him to face up to the hated needle and, as he put it, 'volunteer to be poisoned' over and over again.

That autumn he also had to deal with the news that Peggy Angus had died, aged eighty-nine. He and his siblings missed her. Furlongs had been the focus of so many of their family gatherings down the years, and Peggy herself, artistic, opinionated, encouraging, had been a strong link to the world of their parents – the nearest thing they had to a grandmother.

As the chemotherapy began to bite, James lost his hair and suffered some of the other usual side effects but, luckily, though he was weakened, he didn't feel too sick. That first course improved things considerably. When it was over, he recovered enough to be put on pills for a while instead of injections, though he still had checks every few months. By the next summer he could begin to think again about all the things he wanted to achieve while he had the energy and time.

One of these was another book of his work. Beaford had done nothing with the archive in the five years since he left, so now he wanted to publish an up-to-date collection from it with perhaps some of his private colour work too. The Scolar Press, which had published *The Heart of the Country* fifteen years before, no longer existed, so we took the proposal to Westcountry Books, a publisher in Tiverton. It was warmly received, though we had to put what seemed to us a large amount of money, £10,000, into the first print run (and another £3,500 for further copies later on), taking out a loan from the bank to do it. That meant using our precious nest-egg, James's share of his father's work, as security. I found this alarming in our circumstances, but we were promised quick returns. The book, *A Corner of England*, published in 1995, did sell well locally, but it was a disappointment to James. He had been led to expect high-quality reproduction for our money but the print quality was dull.

Meanwhile, Ben had moved on to sixth form college in Barnstaple for A levels. Having inherited James's scientific and technical genes, his interests were astronomy and IT. In 1992 he left home for astrophysics at Leicester University, and would move on to a career in website development, and an interest in photography. Ella's field was art. She would depart in a few years' time for Falmouth College, and has since maintained the family connection by working at the V&A as curator in the Word and Image Department, in the Print Room that meant so much to James and his father.

In 1997, the lymphoma began to reassert itself. Test results were not good, and there were two courses of chemotherapy over the following year. But they weren't working well enough, and James's heart reacted to them badly, so eventually a course of radiotherapy was tried. He was sent down to the Royal Devon and Exeter Hospital to live in protective isolation for three weeks, which was torture for him as he hated to be alone when he was low. Yet another course of chemo followed, three successive days once a month. He became very rundown, and got shingles.

In the last couple of years he had scoured the internet on the subject of lymphomas and had been given hope by the new type of treatment making waves in America, monoclonal antibodies, drugs which target cancer cells without harming others, and are therefore much kinder to the sufferer. This had been used successfully on some lymphoma patients in the States. He lobbied his specialist eagerly for it, but it was not yet licensed in Britain, and very expensive. By the time he was allowed to have some, it was too late. But here I should acknowledge, gratefully, that the NHS must have spent a huge amount of money on him overall in those last six years – on the fourteen CT scans he had, plus two MRIs, radiography, forty-three days of chemotherapy, five treatments of those antibodies and innumerable blood tests, not to mention hospital accommodation and all the human care.

However, there were good things still in store for him. In the 1980s we had met a photographer called John Batten who knew Devon well, and was a fan of James's work. John was a member of the Royal Photographic Society's Publications Group, and became editor of their series of monographs, one of which featured James. This came out in 1989, and was a very helpful promotion. Now it led to the RPS giving James an Honorary Membership 'for distinguished service to photography', as well as a big retrospective exhibition, *An English Eye,* which they put on for him in 1997. It was curated by photography lecturer, writer and publisher, Peter Hamilton, whose respect and admiration for James's work was a huge boost to him, at a time when he was depressed and drained by prolonged chemotherapy. Peter's support continued for the rest of James's life, and beyond. For the exhibition the two of them spent long hours going through every negative James had taken, archive and private, to make the selection, and working on it revitalised him. Its success was one of the chief rewards of his career.

The other was Peter's book of the same title, published by Devon Books (a short-term partnership of Westcountry Books and Devon County Council), which accompanied the exhibition and which, re-issued by the Bardwell Press,

James and Robin, Western House, Chulmleigh, 1998
Peter Hamilton

has been the main information source on James's work ever since. He and Peter worked on it together with equal enthusiasm, and Peter wrote a most useful text, both personal and technical, as well as overseeing its excellent reproduction values. Two years later, in the spring of 1999, he also recorded interviews with James for the National Sound Archive's Oral History of British Photography project.[10] Though not on his best form by then, James was still his idiosyncratic self.

One of the book's readers was the great man Cartier-Bresson himself, by then in his nineties. Peter Hamilton, who knew him, had sent him a copy. James was touched to get a shakily hand-written card, but a little crestfallen by its message. It read, 'Dear James Ravilious many thanks for sending me your book "An English Eye" – it tastes like a jolly good cup of tea sincèrement votre sincerely yours Henri Cartier-Bresson.' This was not, on the face of it, very complimentary, but we were comforted later on to discover that he was an ardent Anglophile, and very fond of tea.

The RPS *English Eye* exhibition consisted of over a hundred images in assorted sizes, five of them 25" × 39", the prints standing up magnificently to that amount of enlargement from negatives not much bigger than a large postage stamp. They included a number of James's private photographs, of France and elsewhere, which had seldom been exhibited before.

Neither Beaford nor other North Devon bodies could help with sponsorship, but Devon County Council generously paid for the framing. The DCC had long valued James's work and supported it with grants to Beaford. Simon Timms of its Environment Department, who was a friend and admirer, continued to obtain County Council help for him from time to time after the Beaford job ended – with a commission to record some of the historic farmsteads of North Devon, and with the publishing of his later books. Simon has remained one of the archive's staunchest supporters.

The show filled the RPS's large exhibition space in the Octagon at Bath, and later toured to London, the West Country and elsewhere. At the Bath private view, a collector ordered forty-two prints. Reviewers were enthusiastic, too. Alan Bennett wrote in the *New Statesman*: 'these photographs . . . anything but nostalgic, . . . reveal the persistence of an England one had thought long gone . . .' And in mentioning Eric, he added: 'father and son in their different modes both superb exponents of the Englishness of English art.' Later, Sarah Kent wrote in *Time Out*: 'His images look as if they were taken in the 1950s, but Ravilious is not fabricating a romantic idyll. Respect rather than nostalgia informs these marvellous pictures, and a superb eye for composition makes each one an understated delight.'

In the autumn of 1997 there was a merciful pause between treatments when we suddenly felt we should seize the chance of a holiday in spite of everything. France was the obvious destination. We chose Burgundy as neither of us knew it, and because I had always wanted to see the countryside that Colette had written about so lyrically.

We took an early train up from Devon, and then the Eurostar to Paris. There we spent a horrible night as James had such an energy crash that I was convinced we would have to turn back, or even find a hospital. But next morning he revived. France was working its usual magic on him. He insisted on showing me St Denis cathedral, which was one of his favourites, even though it meant crossing Paris by Metro twice. In the afternoon we travelled south by train to Auxerre. James was no longer able to carry suitcases, and needed frequent sits as we walked about, but he was excited as always by the light and the people and the buildings, especially the extraordinary Romanesque crypt beneath the cathedral – a dark and powerfully mediaeval space filled with thick, stunted columns.

From Auxerre we moved on to Vézelay where James could barely climb its long steep street, but the view from the plateau at the top, and the twelfth-century tympanum above the door of the basilica showing a huge gentle Christ commissioning the work of the Apostles, were our reward. We hauled ourselves up again next day to see a wedding there. James had got permission to photograph the wedding party in that magnificent setting.

Finally, we stayed in Joigny, a small wine-producing town on the banks of the River Yonne, where the houses were half-timbered and rendered in brown. The grape harvest was beginning on the surrounding hills, and there were Impressionist scenes going on all along the river bank, especially in an extraordinary mile-long avenue parallel to the river, where strolling figures took the air and made elegant compositions. Despite the heat, James haunted it all day long. He could still forget everything but the scene before him when he had a camera in his hands.

A month after our return a scan revealed new trouble and it was back to chemotherapy again. However, another book was now in prospect, a collaboration with our great friend Peter Beacham, then South West Historic Buildings Inspector for English Heritage and a non-stipendiary clergyman. James had already supplied some illustrations to a book on local vernacular buildings which Peter had co-written. The new book was *Down the Deep Lanes,* a series of essays by Peter on the 'ordinary' features of the countryside which tend to be taken for granted and not preserved or protected, although they add so much to its character as a whole – another tribute to local distinctiveness. Topics such as chapels, hedge patterns and quarries, and materials such as cob and corrugated iron, would need illustrating. James loved the project, and it was ideal therapy for him because Peter was the perfect companion to work with: compassionate and warm, equally at ease with serious issues and hilarious anecdotes. The two of them made trips together to the buildings and scenes that Peter was writing about so that James could record them; and indulged their shared enthusiasm for exploring lanes and churches, and sampling pub lunches, as they went. With Peter he was still able to laugh.

For some of the illustrations James could draw on photos in the archive, but the rest had to be taken specifically. This was a problem both because winter was coming on, and because he was getting weaker, though he could still drive. When Peter was busy, I accompanied James to supply refreshments, carry the equipment, and keep an eye on his energy levels. He was absolutely determined to fulfil his brief, and not let Peter down. In February of the following year, 1999, we made a somewhat risky foray into Cornwall to capture the china clay workings near St Austell, and various sites on the way. The weather was bitingly cold, and it soon began to snow, which excited James. But I didn't much enjoy having to clutch his coat tails as he leaned out over a lagoon of icy, poison-green water to get the right angle on a spoil heap. He was always fearless in pursuit of a good shot. Some weeks later, the very last picture for the book was taken as he leaned heavily on my shoulder for he could no longer walk without support.

Once again, Peter Hamilton oversaw the design and printing, which was as fine as before; and conferred regularly with James to keep him feeling involved in the production. But the book came out too late for him to see.

By the early summer all sorts of physical things were going wrong for him. Most alarming were the attacks of tachycardia, speeding heart rate, which would come on him suddenly, or wake him in the middle of the night feeling very unnerved. Sometimes the rate was so fast I couldn't distinguish individual beats at all. Visits from emergency doctors in the small hours, and ambulance call-outs, followed; and what with them, and all the usual tests and treatments, life became a sort of blur in transit between Barnstaple and home.

The test results continued to be depressing. It seemed that the swifter-moving Hodgkin's lymphoma which he escaped in 1969 had returned, on top of the Non-Hodgkin's. Though I don't think we consciously accepted the fact, the disease was closing in, and James no longer had the strength to fight it. There was a morning when I looked out from the kitchen window to see him sitting in the greenhouse hunched in grief. We had had bad news once again from a scan, and he was facing yet another course of treatment, with decreasing chance of success, when he was still at a low ebb from the previous one. I rushed out to hold him and he gestured to my rows of little auricula plants on the shelving he had made for them, glowing green in tender morning sunshine. 'It's the light,' he said, through tears. 'It's *so* beautiful!'

To me, the light seemed rather heartless that last summer. Day after day was beautiful. As we raced into Barnstaple with yet another heart scare, the Taw valley would reel past in a golden glow, even through the ambulance's darkened panes, like a Samuel Palmer vision. But it was, like a painting, behind glass. In those final years, ordinary life going on seemed always as if seen through a window – at one remove from the ever-present dread we lived with inside.

The very last photographs James took were of the small crowd which gathered on a hill above Chulmleigh on 11 August to see the solar eclipse. The weather was not ideal, but we were able to watch the great shadow sweeping across the landscape towards us from Dartmoor. The last pleasure in his life was his sixtieth birthday later that month. Ben had come down to see him just before; Ella was still at home; and on the day, his sister Anne, her husband Louis, and cousin Brooke, stayed nearby. James was in and out of bed, but up to entertaining his company much as usual.

A couple of weeks later he was just strong enough to get down to the sitting room sofa briefly to greet two visitors, Rose and Jay Deutsch, directors of the Leica Gallery in New York, who had come over to pick up prints by Humphrey Spender and by him for a joint exhibition of British documentary photography (urban and rural) in their gallery on Broadway that autumn. With dwindling energy, James had been supervising the printing for this, which was carried out for him in his darkroom by an assistant, Alan Winn.

Finally, the pain began and he was quickly put on morphine. From then on he slept a lot, and suffered a great deal less than I had always dreaded he would. But his appetite had faded. On 27 September we made yet another ambulance trip to hospital to try to get some nourishment into him, and early next morning he died in his sleep.

EPILOGUE

AMONG MY FIRST FEELINGS when James died were relief and a kind of gratitude: that he had had relatively little pain; that he had been able to go on *living* almost to the end; and that his work had begun to be properly acknowledged just in time for him. After them came anxiety. His most important work, negatives and copyright, was now entirely in the hands of the Beaford people, who by that time knew little about it or him.

Gareth Keene, then chairman of Beaford's board of management, came to my aid. He had been a friend and admirer of James for some years, and the one person connected to Beaford who went to his distant exhibitions and listened to his problems. He and the board kindly agreed that I should have a say in what might happen to the archive, and we signed an agreement that allows me access to the negatives in order to sell traditional darkroom prints made from them by a skilled printer, Paul Cartwright, in exchange for giving Beaford help and advice on the curation of James's work. We also set up a steering committee of James's supporters in various fields to advise on its future. Gradually, Beaford's management began to realise that it was responsible for something of value to posterity that ought to be cherished and promoted.

James's reputation had been growing in the last years of his life, but slowly. It was the spotlight thrown on an artist's work when he dies, together with increasing public interest in threatened country life, that really began to spread the word about him. The *English Eye* exhibition and book focused this attention. People were asking, 'Why haven't we heard of this work before?' The exhibition came back to me eventually, and I have toured selections from it ever since. It had a very popular outing at the National Theatre in 2009. Both exhibition and book inspired other promotion. I curated a couple of new exhibitions for Beaford. With our son Ben, I set up a James Ravilious website (www.jamesravilious.com),[11] and I began to give talks on his work. Canns Down Press embarked on their excellent series of greetings cards of his images, which have taken his work all over Britain, and to Europe, the USA and Australia. Locals visiting relations in New Zealand were amazed to find Archie Parkhouse staring out at them in gift shops there; his image has travelled a great deal further than he ever did. In 2007 Anson Hartford of Banyak Films made a touchingly elegiac documentary film about James and his surviving subjects entitled *James Ravilious: A World in Photographs.* In 2013 a long-held wish of James's came true when the V&A bought prints for their photography collection. For a while, one of these, of Olive Bennett and her cows, hung on display in their new photography gallery in the same row as a Cartier-Bresson, which would have particularly pleased James.

Meanwhile, attitudes had changed in the funding world, and at the Beaford Centre (now called Beaford Arts). The archive began to get more attention. Martyn Warren, chairman of the trustees, and Mark Wallace, the new director, and his staff became enthusiastic about the archive and were able to find funding to undertake the high-resolution scanning of all of James's 'Best' and 'Good' images, and to make them available on a dedicated Beaford Archive website (www.beaford.org),[12] so that a digital version of James's best work has become accessible to a worldwide audience – far wider than he could have hoped for. And in 2014 Beaford Arts collaborated with Plymouth University to mount a large exhibition called *Reflecting the Rural*. Now they have been successful in obtaining a large grant from the Heritage Lottery Fund in order to scan a lot more of James's images and to conserve the negatives. Another part of that plan is an exciting project to record local people talking, especially those who encountered James, so as to add the immediacy of speech to the photographic record. Such recordings of comment and reminiscence, the vernacular history of day-to-day country life in twentieth-century England, could enrich the visual collections, and create the unique and vibrant 'destination' we hoped for for so long, but online instead of in bricks and mortar.

Having a digital presence is not of course the same thing as a physical venue; digital images on a screen, however useful for research, are not completely faithful to a photographer's vision, and have none of the impact of big darkroom prints on a wall – especially in the case of a photographer like James, whose print quality is one of his most admired attributes. I'm hopeful that there will be a home for a major collection of his prints in the future.

Nowadays, James's work is admired by photographers and cinematographers for its technical and compositional skills. Viewers in general warm to the humanity evident in his relationships with his subjects. The portrait of a world remembered from childhood, and thought by many to be long gone, moves people from all sorts of backgrounds – to tears sometimes.

Some find it hard to believe that his pictures were taken since the Second World War, let alone in the 1970s and '80s. Others assume his choice of subjects was very selective, giving a view of the area that was deliberately old-fashioned (and perhaps not very flattering) even at the time when he was making it. It is true that he *concentrated* on the traditional, because it was changing before his eyes, and it was a major part of his brief to capture it before it disappeared. It is also true that he tended to find an old farm more appealing to photograph than a crisply new housing estate. Like many visual people, he enjoyed mess and decay and irregularity. For him such subjects had a human resonance, too: they were eloquent about the past. Both of us were moved by old scenes and buildings; by the continuity of life in our region linking back to its distant past and ticking quietly on 'though dynasties pass'; and by the sense of all the lives that had been lived there before ours. The landscape is still shaped by the anonymous hands that worked it down the centuries. The steps and floors and latches are worn by those who played, loved, endured and died there, leaving little other record of themselves beyond living memory, which is only about three generations long at best, and a few brief entries in the ledgers of their parish church. Those people must have been just as real and complex and absorbing as their descendants whose world James documented in such depth.

But James was not anti-modern. He didn't at all restrict himself to the old and dilapidated. He recorded a great many 'modern' aspects of local life: factories and businesses, the Appledore shipyards, and the building of the A361 – the new road which would open up this countryside to the M5 motorway and the world beyond. He took street life, shops, trades, costume, vehicles, religious and secular events and, in those pre-regulation days, institutions such as schools and hospitals. Many of those subjects are now becoming historic in their turn.

In the eighteen years since James's death, change has accelerated just as John Lane predicted. Though the countryside is still beautiful in many places, farm buildings and machinery have doubled in size; more and more farm work is carried out in the isolation of an enclosed tractor cab, or an office; some of the cows are even being milked by robots. Hay and straw now go into huge black plastic bags, and other crops are covered in miles of white plastic sheeting. Many small trades and their premises have been swallowed up by supermarkets. The traditional pannier markets have been increasingly commercialised. Wind turbines are appearing like exotic toadstools out of the tousled green quilting that James cherished – though I suspect he would have found

them rather intriguing, visually – while satellite dishes and solar panels have sprouted on the roofs of most villages. Locals can now Skype their descendants in Vancouver, Melbourne and Hong Kong. They are closer to the other side of the world than Archie's generation was to their county town, Exeter; though they sometimes say with sadness that they feel like strangers in their own village because of the influx of new faces. For me, the image of James's which heralds that change better than any other is the one of two small boys at Dolton primary school's open day in 1985 demonstrating the school's first BBC Micro computer to a grandmother. That quiet little scene highlights one of the biggest changes in human life in the last hundred years, and perhaps the first time in history when the young could teach the old about something of such huge significance.

Building the new road into North Devon,
near South Molton, 1988
James Ravilious/Beaford Archive

234

James tried to anticipate what would disappear first, and what would be of most interest in the future, knowing how the passage of time can lend a sentimental glow to even the most disturbing innovation. (Some day those controversial wind turbines may seem as quaint and endearing to our descendants as the once-dreaded steam engines do to us.) As Mary Webb, the Shropshire novelist, once wrote: 'We are tomorrow's past.' In everyday life it is easy to forget this important fact, but James's record is a compelling reminder.

In his best work there is a quality of datelessness. As Richard Mabey, reviewing *The Heart of the Country* in *The Countryman* in 1980, commented: 'His pictures have that paradoxical quality of the very finest photographs of being timeless, of suggesting not just the wealth of history leading up to that snatched moment, but that life goes on after the shutter has closed.'

Boys demonstrating the new BBC computer,
Dolton Primary School, 1985
James Ravilious/Beaford Archive

From the social history point of view the two archives together, the images from around 1900, and James's seventeen-year coverage in the 1970s and '80s, all taken in one small piece of countryside, make a portrait of rural life which appears to be unique in Europe in its range and depth. In it, people, places, practices and events can be monitored over eighty or ninety years. The fact that relationships were so interwoven in this district at that time, and that James recorded personal names so assiduously – his people are identifiable individuals, not just rural types and characters – gives the collection the intimacy of a huge family album. This appeals to the increasing number of people who want to research their ancestry on the internet, to students of social history and photography, as well as to a wider public that just feels nostalgic about country life in general. I hope that other detailed observations will document this special place at intervals in the future.

*

People who know James's story think of it with sadness. He did have a good many troubles, and his working life as a photographer was relatively short. But his many friends remember that, in company, he was usually enthusiastic, warm and spontaneously funny – not at all a tragic figure. For the final, most important, thing to say about him is that, in spite of those troubles, he absolutely loved making the archive – stitching his tapestry – and felt himself privileged to have been able to do it. Out with his camera on a Devon morning in spring, with the early light painting a soft bloom on the landscape and the air trembling with birdsong, he would exclaim, 'My God, is this *work*?!'

Highampton churchyard, early morning, 1998
James Ravilious

ACKNOWLEDGEMENTS

MY LOVING THANKS go to my sister, Frances Whistler, for her generous and patient help with my text; and to my children, Ben and Ella, for the moral and practical support they have given me in this, and in so many other projects. I also want to thank James's sister, Anne Ullmann, for helping me with family photos, correspondence and her own memories; and James's cousin, Brooke Calverley, and Joanna Bawden, for sharing their reminiscences.

I'm very grateful to Chris Chapman, Peter Hamilton and George Tucker for their advice on photographic matters, and for the use of their photographs; and to Tony Foster for telling me about his adventures with James; and to Peter Roseveare, David Heald, Michael Johnstone and Richard Bawden, and Gina Warboys of the Old Bedfordians Club, for their help with my research into James's schooldays. I would also like to thank Josephine Bayliss, Marion Ogilvey and Wendy Morrison for their memories of James at St Martin's School of Art and Hammersmith College of Further Education.

In fact I want to thank all the friends, Devonians and others, who have talked to me so warmly about him over the years; and all the people in official positions who befriended and helped him during his photographic career.

I would particularly like to thank Paul Cartwright, who has printed James's photographs with such care since 2005.

My thanks go to the Royal Institute of British Architects for kind permission to reproduce Edwin Smith's lovely photographs of the Ravilious family, and to Robert Organ, artist, and champion of James, for allowing me to quote his introduction to the catalogue for *Living Country*, an exhibition featuring James's work, which was mounted at the Brewhouse Theatre, Taunton, in 2002.

I would also like to thank the Newnham College Archive, Cambridge, for permission to quote from Olive Cook's article on James, 'A Triumph of Evocation', in the journal *Matrix*, 1999.

I am very grateful to the trustees and director of Beaford Arts for kindly allowing me free use of James's images from the Beaford Archive.

Lastly, I would like to acknowledge, with gratitude, the debt we owe to the first director of the Beaford Centre, John Lane (1930–2012), for having the vision to set up the Beaford Archive, and for giving James the chance to find his true vocation.

ROBIN RAVILIOUS

2017

NOTES AND SOURCES

1. Conversation with Sir Vidiadhar Naipaul, Oxford, 1992.
2. Ted Hughes, Preface, *Moortown Diary*, Faber & Faber, 1989.
3. Ibid.
4. Robert Organ, Preface, *Living Country*, exhibition catalogue, Brewhouse Theatre & Arts Centre, 2002.
5. Note on the Black Line: James wished his Beaford Archive images to be printed with the surrounding line, for reasons given in this chapter. However, he was less insistent on it for his private images.
6. Henri Cartier-Bresson, interviewed by Yvonne Baby for *Harper's Magazine*; extracts reprinted in *Leica Photografie*, No. 4, 1964.
7. Olive Cook, 'A Triumph of Evocation', article in *Matrix*, No. 19, 1999 (© Newnham College Archive, Cambridge).
8. Samuel Palmer, *Letters*, ed. A. H. Palmer, 1892.
9. Ibid.
10. Peter Hamilton's interviews with James are in the National Sound Archive's Oral History of British Photography, British Library, 1999.
11. For biographical detail, and a gallery of Beaford Archive and private photographs.
12. For 1,700 of James's best photographs for the Beaford Archive. Many more of his 'lesser' images – those he rated only 'Fair' as photographs, but which are of interest from the social history point of view – will be made available online by the Beaford Archive in the next few years.

SELECT BIBLIOGRAPHY

d'Anjou, René, Duc, *Le Livre du Cueur d'Amours Espris,* 1457, facsimile with introduction and commentary by F. Unterkircher, Thames & Hudson, 1975

Beacham, Peter, *Down the Deep Lanes*, Devon Books, 2000

Bewick, Thomas, *Vignettes*, ed. Iain Bain, Scolar Press, 1978

Bolt, Margaret R., *When we came to Week*, Edward Gaskell, Bideford, 2001

Chapman, Chris, *Wild Goose and Riddon: The Dartmoor Photographs of Chris Chapman*, Devon Books, 2000

Cook, Olive and Edwin Smith, *English Cottages and Farmhouses,* Thames & Hudson, 1960

Garwood, Tirzah, *Long Live Great Bardfield – The Autobiography of Tirzah Garwood (1908–1951)*, ed. Anne Ullmann, Fleece Press, 2012

Hamilton, Peter, *An English Eye – The Photographs of James Ravilious*, Devon Books, 1997

Hoskins, Prof. W. G., *Devon*, David & Charles, Newton Abbot, 1972

Hughes, Ted, *Moortown Diary,* Faber & Faber, 1989

Kitson, Michael, *Claude Lorrain: Liber Veritatis*, British Museum Publications, 1978

Lister, Raymond, *Samuel Palmer and his Etchings,* Faber & Faber, 1969

Morpurgo, Michael, *All Around the Year*, John Murray, 1979

Powers, Alan, *Eric Ravilious: Artist and Designer*, Lund Humphries, 2014

Ravilious, James, *A Corner of England*, Devon Books, 1995

Ravilious, James and Robin, *The Heart of the Country*, Scolar Press, 1980

Russell, James, *Peggy Angus: Designer, Teacher, Painter,* Antique Collectors' Club, 2014

Russell, James, *RAVILIOUS*, Philip Wilson, 2015

Whistler, Laurence, *The Initials in the Heart*, Rupert Hart Davis, 1964

Whistler, Laurence, *The Image on Glass,* John Murray, 1975

Whistler, Laurence, *The Laughter and the Urn – The Life of Rex Whistler,* Weidenfeld & Nicholson, 1985

INDEX

Numbers in *italics* refer to illustration captions